What We Talk About When We Talk About Dumplings

Edited by John Lorinc

Introduction by Karon Liu
Illustrations by Meegan Lim

COACH HOUSE BOOKS, TORONTO

first edition

Published with the generous assistance of the Canada Council for the Arts and the Ontario Arts Council. Coach House Books also acknowledges the support of the Government of Canada through the Canada Book Fund and the Government of Ontario through the Ontario Book Publishing Tax Credit.

LIBRARY AND ARCHIVES CANADA CATALOGUING IN PUBLICATION

Title: What we talk about when we talk about dumplings / edited by John Lorinc.
Names: Lorinc, John, editor.
Identifiers: Canadiana (print) 20220194769 | Canadiana (ebook) 20220194858 | ISBN 9781552454527 (softcover) | ISBN 9781770567474 (EPUB) | ISBN 9781770567481 (PDF)
Subjects: LCSH: Dumplings. | LCSH: Dumplings—Social aspects. | LCSH: Dough.
Classification: LCC TX769 .W43 2022 | DDC 641.81/5—dc23

What We Talk About When We Talk About Dumplings is available as an ebook: ISBN 978 1 77056 747 4 (EPUB), 978 1 77056 748 1 (PDF)

Purchase of the print version of this book entitles you to a free digital copy. To claim your ebook of this title, please email sales@chbooks.com with proof of purchase. (Coach House Books reserves the right to terminate the free digital download offer at any time.)

Table of Contents

Preface

John Lorinc, editor

Dumplings, to state the obvious, are everywhere: supermarket freezers, dim sum trolleys, street food stalls, the menus of eclectic restaurants. Every big city with a half-decent food scene and an influx of newcomers or visitors provides a multiplicity of options from all over the world. They are, and have become, something of an emblem of twenty-first-century global culinary culture – populist, in the good sense of that fraught word, flavourful, and comforting.

'Pillows of happiness,' the late Anthony Bourdain said of xiaolongbao – Shanghai soup dumplings – in a 2014 episode of *Parts Unknown*. 'There are a lot of reasons to come to China,' he said, 'but these things alone are worth the trip.'

Perhaps Bourdain was also drawn to dumplings because their basic culinary architecture is so straightforward (though not always easy to cook): a filling consisting of spiced meat, seafood, leftovers, or veggies encased in dough wrappers of varying consistencies. They can be boiled, baked, steamed, fried, or some combination of the above. Certain types of dumplings eschew the filling altogether, opting instead to absorb flavour from the surrounding soup, sauce, or stew, while others incorporate filling-like elements directly into the dough.

It strikes me that dumplings are to cuisine what birds are to the animal kingdom – astonishing in their variety, migratory, and, well, ancient. Bits of ossified dumpling have turned up in archaeological digs, and there are references in texts dating back millennia, well before the Silk Road trade routes that propagated dumplings across Central Asia and Europe.

For example, a Chinese physician and healer who lived in the second century of the common era is said to have invented wontons. Another Chinese writer, Shu Xi (c. 264–304), described dumplings in a text entitled 'Rhapsody on *bing*,' which includes a reference to 'mantou' – a word of Turkic origin, according to food anthropologist E. N. Anderson, that would have been known across Central Asia. In Greece, Armenia, and Turkey, mantou becomes manti – the tiny, square meat-filled dumplings served with yogurt during celebrations like weddings. Several thousand kilometres east, mantou evolves into mandu – Korean dumplings.

Indeed, the dumpling family tree is nothing if not a testament to the way people have migrated across the globe since time immemorial. Russian pelmeni, which may have originated in Siberia, bear a striking resemblance to tortellini. Georgian khinkali are almost identical in their structure to Bourdain's beloved soup dumplings, except they contain meat. Empanadas, Cornish pasties, and Jamaican patties also seem to derive from a common ancestor.

While culinary historians and anthropologists have documented the progress of what might be described as the dumpling diaspora, the details and precise circumstance can remain a bit fuzzy, not surprisingly, and also hotly contested. Did Marco Polo introduce ravioli to China, or did he bring back dumplings that would inspire pasta? Depends on who you ask.

Some accounts are more precise, however. Gyoza, the ubiquitous Japanese pork-and-cabbage dumpling, derives from jiaozi, the original Chinese version, in a very specific way. After World War II, Japanese soldiers returned from China with recipes for gyoza they'd eaten while stationed there, *The Guardian* explains in a 2019 story about a city at the centre of Japan's booming gyoza industry. The country's post-war economy lay in ruins, and food shortages, including rice, were severe, although U.S. wheat could be imported. '"They were easy to make, nutritious, and none of the ingredients were particularly hard to get hold of," says Akihiro Suzuki, secretary general of the Utsunomiya Gyoza Association, which represents 96 of the city's estimated 200 gyoza restaurants.' After decades of tweaking and experimentation, gyoza can no longer be described as derivative of a Chinese dumpling, but rather a specialized Japanese dish in its own right. In a curious twist, imports of contaminated gyoza mass-produced in Chinese food processing factories in 2008 caused hundreds to fall ill and exposed the lingering tensions in relations between the two countries.

'Everyone's got a dumpling story,' my friend and collaborator Tatum Taylor Chaubal said when I texted her about contributing an essay to this anthology. And, of course, she's right. In fact, this book's principal ingredient is the notion that dumplings are not only universal, but frequently woven into the fabric of our lives in interesting and complicated ways.

Some important disclosures about what follows: this is not a cookbook, although it does contain some recipes. The contributors include talented professional food writers and chefs, but also essays from people who don't normally write about food. The title, a riff on the lead short story in a 1981 collection by Raymond Carver, expresses the idea that with dumplings, context is a critical element. Yes, millions of people every day scarf down dumplings without thinking twice about the significance of these foods. Yet, as the stories in here show, dumplings – and dumpling-making, in particular – turn up at critical junctures, especially those moments when knowledge and emotion pass from one generation to the next.

This collection does not aspire to be comprehensive. The list below – which is partial and doesn't include all the sub- and sub-sub-varieties, not to mention those versions unique to individual families – illustrates the scope and diversity of the dumpling genus. In compiling the anthology, I did not spend a lot of time worrying about cultural appropriation, as one could say that the history of dumplings is, in its essence, a 2000-year-old exercise in unceasing appropriation and innovation, for which everyone who enjoys eating may be grateful.

Finally, a word about the definition: *what is a dumpling?* In her essay, Michal Stein describes how she and a group of friends tackled this riddle, attempting to come up with a framework and a taxonomy. In fact, I can say that almost everyone who heard about the anthology when it was still in the oven began by posing this exact question. My own view is that the debate about the answer is much more fun and flavourful than some fixed set of parameters, although others might disagree. Yet guardrails are important, so some foods that could be described as 'dumpling adjacent' – e.g., pies, wraps, tacos, calzone, etc. – didn't make the cut. That said, you could argue it both ways … perhaps over dim sum.

A NOT-AT-ALL-COMPLETE LIST OF DUMPLINGS
AROUND THE WORLD

ASIA
Shumai (China)
Har Gow (China)
Char Siu Bao (China)
Zongzi (China)
Wonton (China)
Guotie/Potstickers (China)
Baozi (China)
Xiaolongbao (Shanghai)
Bánh Nậm (Vietnam)
Bánh Tet (Vietnam)
Momo (Nepal, Tibet, India)
Shabhaley (Tibet)
Dango (Japan)
Mochi (Japan)
Gyoza (Japan)
Mandu (Korea)
Khinkali (Georgia)
Samosa (India)
Pakora (India)
Gulab Jaman (India)
Modak (India)
Pelmeni (Russia)
Boraki (Armenia)

NORTH AMERICA
Glissants (Quebec)
Grandpères (Quebec)
Drop Dumplings (Métis Nation)
Cornmeal Dumplings (U.S. South)
Apple Dumplings (Pennsylvania)
Chicken and Dumplings (U.S. South)
Panki' alhfola' (Chickasaw Nation)
Matzo Balls (Central Europe/U.S.)

CENTRAL/SOUTH AMERICA
Tamales (Mexico)
Spinners (Jamaica)
Soup Dumplings (Trinidad, Jamaica)
Jamaican Patty (Jamaica)
Bolon de Verde (Ecuador)
Empanadas (Chile/Argentina)
Coxinha (Brazil)
Pastel (Brazil)
Papas Rellenas (Peru)

EUROPE
Tortellini (Italy)
Ravioli (Italy)
Gnocchi (Italy)
Rissóis (Portugal)
Knedlíky (Czechia)
Quenelles (France)
Cornish Pasties (England)
Pierogi (Poland)

Vareniki (Ukraine)
Pitepalts (Sweden)
Kroppkakor (Sweden)
Kartoffelkloesse (Germany)
Szilvás Gombóc (Hungary)
Kreplach (Central Europe)

MIDDLE EAST/AFRICA
Manti (Turkey)
Shish Barak (Lebanon)
Awameh (Middle East)
Madombi (Botswana)
Dombolo (South Africa)
Souskluitjies (South Africa)
Fufu (West Africa/Caribbean)

OCEANIA
Dimmies (Australia)
Batagor (Indonesia)
Chai Kueh (Indonesia)
Pangsit Goreng (Indonesia)
Siomay (Indonesia)
Siopao (Phillipines)

Introduction

Karon Liu

I've been a Toronto-based food writer for more than a decade, and there's one project I've always wanted to do but never got around to (so far). I've wanted to map out this city of almost six million people through dumplings. My map would show the different enclaves and communities based on where all the pierogi places are versus the locations of the wonton soup restaurants or all the manti spots.

Toronto is the perfect city to create such a map: a metropolis that has evolved to be one of the most diverse culinary destinations in the world, thanks to waves of migration resulting in cuisines from disparate parts of the world commingling with each other. This place is a mix of cooks practising centuries-old techniques learned from previous generations, innovators sharing new creations in the age of TikTok, and cooks embracing their third-culture cooking – combining what they learned from their parents with the new flavours and methods that come from living in a city where a roti spot, a sushi restaurant, and a souvlaki joint can all be found in a single plaza.

A perfect example of this phenomenon is Tibet Kitchen in Little Tibet, a strip of Tibetan-owned restaurants and shops in Toronto's Parkdale neighbourhood. Chaat momos are one of my favourite local dishes: these Tibetan meat dumplings (or veggie, depending on my mood) are smothered in a vibrant orange tamarind sauce, then sprinkled with chopped tomatoes, cilantro, yogurt, and crispy sev, combining Tibetan and Indian flavours; that's an example of fusion done right – the flavours and textures work so well in every bite.

The more I write about food, the more I come to realize that such an undertaking requires a team of people. Yes, dumplings are universal – it's why they're such an easy entry-way into a culture's cuisine. At the same time, there are so many dumpling variations: steamed, fried, or boiled; filled or not; sweet or savoury; big or small; in soups or on their own. There are nuances to cuisines that vary between regions, cities, and – heck – households and generations that no one person can ever fully grasp.

Technically, the matzo balls in Ashkenazi Jewish cooking, the xiaolongbao or soup dumplings in Shanghainese cuisine, and Jamaican spinners used in soups and stews are all categorized as dumplings. But there's not a lot else these dishes have in common – aside from their deliciousness. I remember being introduced to spätzle as a teen, when I was invited to a friend's home to try Austrian home cooking. I gobbled the spätzle along with the schnitzel, perplexed but mind-blown that dumplings existed beyond the wontons I ate growing up.

Heck, even with the wontons, everyone in my friends' and family's circles prefers a different filling or fold. One friend prefers the squeeze method – literally putting a bit of filling into the wrapper and then squeezing her hand into a fist to seal it – because that's the fastest method (and most common among sifus at restaurants). My mom, meanwhile, prefers the fold that makes the dumpling look like a person wearing a bonnet 'cause that's what her mom taught her. Don't even get me started on the differences between a wonton, a water dumpling, a potsticker, and a soup dumpling … mostly because I'm still learning the different techniques and regional variations of each of these as I dive ever deeper into Chinese cooking.

To be a good food writer is to know that there's no way one person can be an expert on every cuisine. For me, the best way to encapsulate a snapshot of this hypothetical dumpling map of Toronto is to have more than one contributor, and that's what this book sets out to do.

Every one of the contributors has a different definition of what a dumpling means to them, and that's fantastic.

To live in a city where there's no monoculture or definitive way to define a dish is to be spoiled with a seemingly infinite collection of flavours, culinary knowledge, and memories that people are eager to share.

What I can do is kick-start my hypothetical map with a story about what dumplings mean to me.

For as long as I can remember, when my mom had run out of ideas for dinner and was in a rush, wontons would be one of her go-tos: ground pork, napa cabbage, a mix of dark and light soy sauces with some cane sugar, and a package of store-bought dumpling wrappers. I'd watch her pinch a walnut-sized lump of the filling from a large metal bowl and lay it in the centre of the wrapper. She'd dip a finger into a rice bowl filled with water, swipe the edge of the wrapper, and – through a series of pinches and folds – a dumpling would appear in seconds.

Now a confession: despite all the times I've watched my mom make wontons and promised myself that I'd eventually pick up the skill so I could a) have another quick weeknight dinner meal in my arsenal; and b) gain some street cred as a guy who writes a lot about Chinese food, I have yet to tackle making dumplings on my own.

So I consider myself to be in a culinary grey zone. I'm an experienced food writer whose palate gravitates toward Cantonese cooking. And yet I cannot fold a dumpling to save my life. Does not being able to fold a perfectly neat and symmetrical wonton make me any less of an authority on writing about food?

I remember once attending a dumpling-folding party – this is what happens when you have foodie friends. After a few minutes, I was gently, um, encouraged to do something else because I was basically wasting perfectly good wrappers with every failed attempt. Funnily enough, my Hungarian partner, who had never touched a dumpling wrapper before, was able to crank them out without much effort. Since then, he'll occasionally make a few dozen batches to freeze for future meals. Oddly, the way he folds his dumplings is similar to my mom's technique. I have no idea if this was a secret joint effort between them to goad me into trying to learn again.

In the early months of COVID-19, in January 2020, I went with some friends to a noodle spot in Markham called Wuhan Noodle 1950 to order its dry pot noodles and a side of dumplings. Months before the pandemic emergency was officially declared in Canada, Chinese restaurants had begun to see their business plummet due to old, racist stereotypes about Chinese food and cleanliness, all of which had resurfaced amidst simmering fear about the virus.

This particular place had been inundated with racist prank calls that were perpetuated on social media. Sensing that the eatery could use a positive boost, I went, had a great meal, and wrote about it for the *Toronto Star*. I explained the restaurant's regional Chinese cooking and how a place like this fit into the evolution of Chinese food in the Greater Toronto Area. In recent years, we've seen a greater proliferation of regional Chinese cooking from both independent owners and international chains using the GTA as a test market before expanding elsewhere. The Chinese food here evolved from the Canadian-Chinese chop suey houses to more Hong Kong and Cantonese cooking as the GTA saw an influx of immigrants in the eighties and nineties. Then more people from Mainland China came, bringing their regional cooking – as well as international Chinese chains serving everything from hot pot to different styles of noodles.

Chinese food is no longer lumped into one giant category, and diners are increasingly aware that hand-pulled beef noodles are representative of Lanhzou, and in order to get a steamer basket of xiaolongbao, you have to go to a Shanghainese place. While the circumstances of how I found out about this place serving Wuhan dry pot noodles are unfortunate, it gave me an opportunity to talk about the dish stemming from the Hubei province.

Dumplings popped into my life again during the initial months of the pandemic lockdown in Toronto. Bags of frozen potstickers became a bit of a saviour in my household in the pre-vaccine days of the pandemic, when every trip to the supermarket seemed like running to get supplies during a zombie apocalypse.

We bought frozen potstickers in bags of a hundred from a wholesale shop called the Northern Dumpling Co. in our Scarborough neighbourhood. During the many days in those early months when I could barely get out of bed, let alone cook a meal from scratch, the dumplings kept me fuelled to carry on for another day.

Similarly, in the spring of 2022, church basements and restaurants across Canada churned out varenyky by the thousands to raise relief funds for Ukrainian refugees. Diners wanting to show support ordered the dumplings by the dozens and became more interested in learning about Ukraine's answer to the pierogi.

What I'm trying to say is that everyone has a different relationship when it comes to food, including something as seemingly commonplace and traditional as the dumpling. As people move, generational attitudes and values shift, ingredients and techniques are adapted or evolve, and as technology changes the way we cook, the role food plays in our lives also changes.

It's impossible for a dish to remain static, like a museum showpiece, if the people who cook and eat it aren't static. As a result, there will never be a definitive dumpling guide, whether as a map or an anthology, because our relationship to food never stops changing. Instead, consider this volume a snapshot of how our relationship to dumplings stands at this moment, as told by the people in this moment.

Who knows? Maybe, five years from now, if you ask me what my relationship to dumplings is, I'll be able to say they're one of my go-to, quick weeknight meals. Perhaps I'll add masala spice because an Indian restaurant owner gave me a few jars of his dad's mixes and boasted it could be used in anything. Or I'll add finely chopped mint to the filling as a nod to the Vietnamese restaurants I always turn to for takeout – and as a way to use local ingredients – because I have a serious overgrown mint problem in my yard.

The Wrapper

Around the World

Michal Stein

Sitting in molasses traffic on a Saturday afternoon, all I could think about was the bag full of Tibetan momo in the passenger seat beside me. The smell of meat and chili sauce. No one would notice if one went missing, I thought. The guys at TC Tibetan Momo in Etobicoke had even thrown in some patties for free when I told them I was going to a dumpling party – surely they would be fair game if I needed a snack. But I was forty minutes late to the Dumplings Around the World feast, and the least I could do was arrive with all my contributions intact.

I arrived at Alex's apartment, balancing two orders of momo in one hand and a cooler full of ravioli in the other, plus a plastic bag full of paper plates and napkins. Everyone was already there, waiting for me.

'Finally!' called Alex.

Crowded around an oblong table, we started to lay out the dumplings. I began with my two orders of momo – one beef, one vegetable – the patties, and packs of pickled cabbage.

Beside a pile of chopsticks and forks, and a bowl of sour cream, Miriam set down what looked like a salad, but was in fact individual lettuce leaves containing shredded vegetables, each pocket already dressed.

Erica put out three kinds of pierogies: beef, potato and cheddar, and sweet cheese.

Jordy and Becca, who had flown in from Brooklyn for the occasion, ordered dim sum, which took up the entire lower third of the table: shrimp cakes, barbecue pork buns, fried shrimp balls, har gao, shrimp dumplings, siu mai, red bean cakes, sticky rice wrapped in a banana leaf, xiaolongbao, vegetable dumplings, and rice noodle rolls.

Sarah brought the dish that would become the most controversial of them all: samosa.

With the table nearly full, Brandon squeezed in chicken and vegetable gyoza, plus the coxinha he had picked up on Alex's behalf. Someone balanced a tray of grocery store mochi on the edge.

Due to my late arrival, we had no time to boil Ela's stinging nettle ravioli, so she set it down in its zip-lock bag; she would cook it and toss it with butter after we took the photo.

We adorned the Lazy Susan with hot sauce, soy sauce, and mustard. The table was complete.

Before digging in, Alex snapped a photo from above. I tweeted it out, saying, *We did dumplings around the world.*

By the time I went to bed that night, it had been retweeted 43 times and had 443 likes. Over the next forty-eight hours, it would be shared over 32,000 times, rack up 1,600 comments, and get more than 236,000 likes.

It was April 9, 2022. The pandemic hadn't ended. People felt strongly about dumplings.

One Sunday afternoon in April 2019, a group of my friends and I gathered at Dim Sum King on Dundas Street in Toronto for Julie-Rae King's twenty-eighth birthday. Jordy, a twenty-six-year-old museum manager, brought her new girlfriend,

Becca, a twenty-eight-year-old arts professional, both of them in town from New York. Julie-Rae, who worked in theatre, was there with Alex, her twenty-seven-year-old fiancé from Scotland.

We were tied together by summer camp – Julie-Rae, Jordy, and I had grown up at camp together, first as campers, then as counsellors, and, in Julie's case, eventually running the whole thing. After participating in the same youth movement in the U.K., Alex had joined us as a counsellor. Becca went to a sister camp in Pennsylvania. Other camp friends may have been present for the feast – perhaps Erica, then a twenty-six-year-old medical student, and Ela, a twenty-six-year-old GIS mapper. But they weren't sure whether they were actually present for that 2019 lunch or if we had just talked about it so much that it had become part of our collective memory.

We spent hours waving down the carts, watching for our favourites – siu mai, har gao, cheung fun. After stuffing ourselves to the point that we were more dim sum than human, the conversation turned to dumplings.

There we were – a group of Jews, sitting around, eating a lot of pork and shrimp. As unkosher as it gets. And yet, as someone held up a shrimp dumpling, the question arose: could kreplach, the solemn dumpling of our shtetl ancestors, find a place at the dim sum table?

From kreplach, we moved to pierogi. Could one serve pierogi at dim sum? True, pierogies were accompanied by sour cream, not soy sauce. But they shared an undeniable common formula: meat or vegetables, wrapped in dough, then steamed, boiled, or fried. Gyoza. Tibetan momo. Ravioli. Tortellini. Samosa. Was a calzone a dumpling?

Every culture, we concluded, had its own signature dumpling.

We set ourselves a mission: one day, we would gather as many different dumplings as we could find and set off on a culinary voyage of dumplings around the world. We would reconvene one year later, for the occasion of Julie-Rae's twenty-ninth birthday: April 7, 2020.

Just over two years later, on a hot Saturday in late August 2021, I was sitting in Alex's apartment with that same group of friends, the air conditioner running on high. Julie-Rae's absence hung heavily in the room. After suffering a sudden pulmonary embolism two weeks earlier, she had slipped into a coma and never woke up. She died that Wednesday, and the funeral had been held the day before.

Jordy and Becca were back in town, too. In a series of events that felt like a badly written soap opera, Jordy's mother died the same morning Julie had been rushed to the hospital. Between the two deaths, our little group spent most of August becoming expert shiva attendees.

Technically, there's no shiva on a Saturday, the Sabbath, but we wanted to be together to make sure Alex wasn't alone. We called it a 'Speakeasy Shiva' – no grown-ups allowed, no strange relatives, no random congregation members eager to get the afternoon prayers started. Just the group of friends in their late twenties and early thirties trying to understand how it was possible that Julie-Rae, the friend we could always count on to organize our get-togethers, wasn't there to organize this one.

But for the Speakeasy Shiva's raison d'être, it would have been a pretty good party. We couldn't quite figure out how many people were going to come. Ten? Eighteen? Twenty-five? I had picked up a few pancake boxes from Emma's Country Kitchen and made two blueberry-peach French toast casseroles.

Friends we hadn't seen since before the pandemic began to arrive, and we spent hours looking at photos and telling stories. As the afternoon wore on and the party waned, a few of us piled onto the sectional couch in the living room, kicking Alex's languid dog, Daisy, out of the prime corner spot.

'Jules never got her Dumplings Around the World birthday,' someone said.

Born in April, Julie-Rae had two pandemic birthdays in deep lockdown. A year and a half into the pandemic, it felt like ages since we'd been able to properly spend time together. Like everyone else, all our celebrations had been kicked down the road. We assumed that one day we'd be able to throw everyone a birthday party that would make up for the ones spent on Zoom. Julie and Alex postponed their wedding – twice – in the hopes that they'd be able to have a full celebration with friends and family, including Alex's from Scotland.

In the weeks before Julie's death, we had all gotten the second dose of the vaccine, and Covid numbers were going down. We were finally starting to figure out how to be together again, rediscovering the joy of going to each other's apartments to eat takeout and watch movies. Julie had a short glimpse of that world, but was never feted in the way she deserved.

And so we decided we would do Dumplings Around the World, in her memory, for her birthday.

But this raised the question we had debated over dim sum way back in 2019: what constitutes a dumpling?

Let us begin with what we know. There's dim sum: shrimp dumplings, shrimp and chive dumplings, soup dumplings. This gives us a starting point – meat or vegetables, wrapped in a single piece of dough, then boiled, steamed, or fried.

Pierogi, kreplach, tortellini, and Tibetan momo all fit the criteria, too.

Would a Scotch egg count as a dumpling? It is a food (boiled egg) wrapped in an edible casing (sausage and bread crumbs), then fried. A calzone, though much larger in size, fits the same description.

By that logic, one could also call turducken a dumpling – it's a deboned chicken, stuffed into a deboned duck, stuffed into a deboned turkey. One person suggested including turducken at Dumplings Around the World.

The room fell silent.

Yes, turducken is food wrapped in other food, but there is something distinctly undumpling-like about a turducken. No, we decided, turducken is not a dumpling, which means a Scotch egg is also probably not a dumpling. A calzone, we concluded, is distinctively a pocket.

My tweet took our extended discourse about what was or was not a dumpling to a global stage. Hundreds of people argued in the comments, thousands more in quote tweets, about what we had missed or gotten wrong in our spread.

Many took issue with our inclusion of one item in particular: the samosa.

This is samosa. Don't complicate it, someone said.

Yes and? they are still technically dumplings, said another.

Are hot pockets dumplings? asked a third.

We're edging close to deep philosophy here, commented a fourth.

We were not the only ones to get lost in the minutiae of what was or was not a dumpling. Being confronted with a table full of them provoked a cycle of emotions among those who responded: first, a feeling of pride for seeing one's dumpling included; then, perhaps, a feeling of frustration upon realizing what we hadn't included; and then finally, a feeling of existential dread about the task of identifying the Platonic form of a dumpling.

It became clear that we had made a crucial error in defining dumplings for ourselves. Size, it turned out, matters. Not only is a dumpling spiced meat or vegetables wrapped in dough, then boiled or fried, it should also be small enough to eat in a bite or two. This probably disqualified the barbecue pork buns we had on our spread, not to mention the rice noodle rolls, which don't even pretend to be dumplings. But to lay out an array of dim sum and *not* include barbecue pork buns would be to deprive ourselves for the sake of semantics.

While plenty of people were hung up on what we got right or wrong about our dumpling selection, a much larger faction were tagging their friends, saying, *Can we do this too?*

Dumplings are a food most pleasurable when eaten with others.

When you're sitting around a table with friends, dumplings serve as a conduit. The act of eating the meal itself becomes as social as the conversation. You order three or four different kinds, then pass them around until everyone is well-fed. The plates become like airplanes, their flight paths criss-crossing the table. You pass, you eat, you pass, you eat … until the plates have made more round-the-world trips than you can count.

And so, the question of whether to go for dumplings becomes a question not only of what you're going to be eating, but how. There will be collaboration, the possibility of surprise and delight, and, of course, the dumplings themselves – edible magnets pulling you closer to your dining companions.

We had become accustomed to eating together a lot during those days in August after Julie-Rae had fallen into a coma.

Every night when Alex came back from the hospital, we had dinner together. We tried to make his apartment feel full and lived-in, knowing that the emptiness would feel deeper once we left for the night. We wanted to wrap ourselves around him, become a protective layer. Eating together wasn't always easy – many of those dinners began with the question of whether we wanted bad news or worse news.

No matter what the news was, we would have to eat at some point. You can't cry with a mouth full of food.

After we finished eating all the dumplings we possibly could during our Dumplings Around the World feast, we began to package up the leftovers for people to take home.

'Jules would have loved this,' Sarah said, tucking samosas into her take-away box. I looked over to the couch, where Daisy lay splayed out in the corner, as if she were digesting a feast of her own.

'She would have been right there, where Daisy is, so full she couldn't move,' I replied.

'She would have eaten too many pierogies and not taken her Lactaid pills,' added Alex.

Though Julie-Rae never got to participate in Dumplings Around the World, we knew her spreadsheet for the event would have been spectacular – everything would have been arranged weeks in advance, and there would have been no question about who was responsible for what. I like to think that even though she wasn't there to organize it, she still made it happen.

'There are no silver linings,' Becca had said that summer at the shiva for Jordy's mother. 'Only moments of grace.'

A few weeks after our Dumplings Around the World feast, I went to New York to visit my sister. I took the opportunity to catch up with Jordy and Becca. It was late afternoon when the three of us walked into the 2nd Ave Deli on East 33rd Street. We were led to the back of the restaurant and into a booth with green vinyl benches. The walls, a combination of wood panelling and white tile with red and green accents, brimmed with old black-and-white framed photos of shtetl-type figures, illuminated by bright white sconces.

We ordered a plate of kreplach for the table and two matzo ball soups, with three cans of Dr. Brown's Cel-Ray soda to wash it down. Our soups arrived in wide, flat bowls, with sliced carrots and celery nestled beneath baseball-sized matzo balls. The broth came in a metal cup, and our server poured it over the matzo balls in front of us. He did both bowls at the same time. It was pretty impressive.

'Very hot,' he said.

We resumed our debate about dumpling taxonomy. Consider the matzo ball: roughly eight centimetres in diameter, impossible to eat in just a bite. The outer layer is fluffy, almost effervescent from the soda water, and then it becomes denser and denser still as the spoon works toward the middle.

As a child, I called this a dumpling, yet it bears no resemblance to the dumplings we had eaten at our Dumplings Around the World feast.

'A classic American-style dumpling is when you take some sort of dough, and you poach it in liquid, and then it floats. Like chicken and dumplings,' said Becca, the resident American. This was true, too, of Caribbean dumplings, and of matzo balls. 'How could you possibly say that this matzo ball is related to a gyoza?' she asked. 'Nothing is wrapped.

They're not even steamed or fried. They're poached.'

'They're boiled,' I responded.

'I would offer that they're poached, because you don't do them at a rolling boil,' Becca said.

'I do,' replied Jordy. 'I keep it really hot for half an hour or forty minutes.'

We kept coming back to the question: how are these dumplings related to the more delicate wrapped varieties of dumplings we had eaten two weeks earlier?

Becca pulled out her phone. 'All right. Origin: English. *Dump*.'

'Like you dump it in soup,' I said.

'In the early seventeenth century, it came from the rare adjective, *dump*, which means, of the consistency of dough,' she read. This accounts for the dumplingness of a matzo ball. It also means that for the filled variety, it's the wrapper – not the filling – that makes it a dumpling.

For dumplings, it seemed, it's what's on the outside that counts.

Our kreplach arrived and, once again, we found ourself face-to-face with food that looks nothing like what we thought of as dumpling. They were bigger than I had expected – about the size of my palm – and the dough had a chewiness to it, as well as a grey pallor that made me want to take it to the doctor. As I cut into it, dry bits of ground beef spilled out.

'This just tastes like the Pale of Settlement,' said Becca.

And yet it met the criteria: here we have meat – barely spiced, but spiced nonetheless – wrapped in dough, then boiled or fried.

'One thing I have taken from this whole Dumplings Around the World process,' said Jordy, 'is that I had a much better and clearer understanding of what a dumpling was before we did any of it.'

And now?

'I have no idea what a dumpling is.'

One could spend hours arguing about what is and isn't a dumpling. There are enough different genres that we could throw an annual Dumplings Around the World party for the next five years without having any repeats. You could put a hot dog in a wonton wrapper and call it a dumpling. You could stuff a Timbit with a strawberry and call it a dumpling. You could wrap M&Ms in a scooped-out bagel and call it a dumpling. The philosophical debates, however, are secondary to the true joy of eating dumplings.

Dumplings are a delicious excuse to while away the afternoon with friends – trying something new, savouring an old favourite, and cherishing hours well-spent sharing food around a table. To gather for dumplings is to celebrate our earthly senses with all their smells, flavours, and textures. But combined with people you love? That's a taste of something truly divine.

For Jules, our heavenly dumpling.

THE DUMPLINGS AROUND THE WORLD MENU

Vegetable Momo
Beef Momo
Tibetan Patty
Salad Dumpling
Cheese and Potato Pierogi
Sweet Cheese Pierogi
Beef Pierogi
Stinging Nettle Ravioli
Vegetable Dumpling
Shrimp Cake
Red Bean Cake
Fried Shrimp Ball
Sticky Rice in Banana Leaf
Barbecue Pork Bun
Shrimp Dumpling
Soup Dumpling
Sweet Egg Custard Bun
Har Gao
Siu Mai
Rice Noodle Roll
Samosa
Chicken Gyoza
Vegetable Gyoza
Mochi
Cheese Coxinha
Chicken Coxinha

michal stein ✔
@MichalStein2

We did dumplings around the world

6:21 PM · Apr 9, 2022 · Twitter for iPhone

22.7K Retweets   **9,725** Quote Tweets   **236.1K** Likes

Siopao Is Not Just for Kids

Christina Gonzales

When chef Angela Dimayuga published *Filipinx: Heritage Recipes from the Diaspora* in late 2021, her recipe for siopao was accompanied by a story from her childhood. Having grown up in a family of six children, she wrote about how she and her older siblings would sneak through the back door of a fortune-cookie factory in San Francisco's Chinatown to watch the assembly line while her mom waited at the bakery to pick up baozi – 'what we call siopao,' Dimayuga wrote. 'We'd buy a dozen with fortunes, and another dozen discards, broken cookies left flat, and unfolded, just to eat, alongside our [buns].'

Most Filipinos, both in the Philippines and abroad, have memories of eating siopao as children. 'I went through a phase as a kid where I only ate the filling,' wrote one food blogger, whose page I scoured for siopao-making tips. But ask even the most avid, non-Filipino restaurant goer and food enthusiast in my city, Toronto, as well as places like New York, Chicago, or Boston, and it's likely they've never even heard the name – pronounced *shoh-pao*.

Why does a Chinese bun filled with a meat dish – originally inherited from Spain, and frozen and sold in plastic packs in the Little Manilas around the globe – exist mostly within the confines of Filipino homes and mouths?

In *Tikim: Essays on Philippine Food and Culture*, the late Filipino food historian Doreen Fernandez explained it best when she wrote, 'Philippine foodways have been difficult even for Filipinos to understand, so variegated they are, coming as they do from different cultural strains … When one asks today, therefore: What is Philippine food? The answer can be neither brief nor simple.'

Siopao is hard to understand because Philippine food culture – forever changed by our history as a colony of both Spain and America – is hard to understand. This steamed dumpling, relatively unknown outside the Filipino community, tells the story of our history through its exact parts: the bun – Chinese ties; the filling – Spanish conquistadors; the means by which we eat it – American culture.

Siopao, in fact, might be the way that you and I can better understand Filipino food.

'Pinch, pinch, pinch,' I mumbled to myself after four already-failed siopaos unravelled before my eyes. I was hovering over the island in my kitchen, trying to be as present as possible; no one told me that closing a dumpling required such focus. My husband looked over at me while reading a book to our son; he'd watched me slog all day over this dough. I'd spent the morning making two batches: the yeast hadn't activated in the first one; the second was perfect. But siopao dough needs to proof three times over the course of a day. And while I'm an avid home cook, I'm practically a dough virgin.

I'd never seen anyone make siopao by hand – not my late mamang (grandmother), or any of my titas (aunts), or my mom. I panic-messaged the Filipino chefs I follow on Instagram: Dennis Tay, chef de cuisine at DaiLo in Toronto, was the most helpful: 'After the first mix, you should let the dough double in size, while covered,' he wrote. 'Then portion it and form it into balls, cover it, and let it double again. And then after you've stuffed, folded, and closed them, you should let it proof again uncovered until the lines from the folds soften a little.'

I was out of my depth. The convenience of frozen siopao was something I'd enjoyed my entire life. The siopao I loved didn't come from the hands of any matriarchs I knew personally, let alone from a bamboo steamer; it came out of a plastic box.

Most people won't know that the commercialization of siopao is an American legacy. Like peeling back the layers of an onion, the story of siopao is revealed – bit by bit – through our history.

Alex Orquiza, a Filipino history professor and author of *Taste of Control: Food and the Filipino Colonial Mentality Under American Rule*, says American advertising for canned goods – and the values like 'cheap, easy, healthy,' which marketers attributed to them – took hold in the Philippines in the 1920s and 1930s. It had been some thirty years since Spain ceded the islands to the United States, and America was profiting. By 1934, the Philippines was the largest market for U.S. exports like cigarettes, soap, and canned milk, and its ninth largest export market overall.

The Philippine middle class in Manila welcomed the canned foods they saw in print and on their televisions. (In fact, Spam, a canned, cooked pork, is still considered a national favourite.) 'Industrialized labour really takes off during that time period and is picked up again after World War II,' said Orquiza over the phone from Boston. 'The fact that Magnolia brand exports [frozen siopao] so we can buy a pack of six here is along the same lines as [Philippine consumers] being ingrained into buying Del Monte canned fruit [from America].'

But long before Americans brought industrialization to a primarily agrarian society, there were the conquistadors. Ferdinand Magellan, a Portuguese explorer, landed in the Philippines in 1521 and claimed it on behalf of Spain. In 1543, the territory was named 'Felipinas' after the crown prince, Don Felipe of Spain, who would later become King Felipe II. The archipelago of over 7,100 islands later became known as Las Islas Felipinas. The anglicized version – the Philippines.

Along with capturing a share of the spice trade in the resource-rich country, Spain's mission was to convert Filipinos to Christianity and also to make connections with China and Japan in order to establish Christian missions there.

From 1565 to 1898, a Spanish colonial government – friars – ruled the country. In his book *A History of the Philippines, from Indios Bravos to Filipinos*, Luis H. Francia so accurately described the way colonialists changed us evermore. (The word *Indios* was what the Spanish called Philippine native peoples. José Rizal, hero of the Philippine nationalist movement, which began in 1863 and culminated in 1898 with the expulsion of Spain, borrowed the term to name his group of intellectuals who called themselves 'Indios Bravos.')

'In a sense we were [also] Indios Bravos ourselves,' Francia writes, describing him and his writer friends in the 1960s, 'not just intensely aware of but embodying the legacies of the Spanish and North Americans, in our lives and ways of thinking, even in our blood – to be wrestled with, confronted, transformed, but not eliminated.'

In the ways in which Filipinos eat, the Spanish influence has not been eliminated but rather transformed. Pork asado – braised, not grilled as the name intends – is a dish originating from Mexico (think: carne asada). In fact, the Spanish expedition to the Philippines in 1565 from New Spain (Mexico), to establish Spain's first colonial government, was part of an effort to build a trade route carrying Chinese silks from the Philippines to Mexico, while shuttling silver, missionaries, and soldiers back to the islands.

Chinese traders have been on the islands since the tenth century, importing Southeast Asian commodities like cotton, coconuts, and woven mats. Under Spain, they migrated in mass numbers from southern China's coastal provinces, like Fujian, Amoy, and Guangdong, to work as craftsmen and artisans. Initially, Spain had placed all of these siong lai (Hokkien for 'frequent visitors,' or 'sangleys,' using the Anglo term) into a Manila ghetto. In 1594, the Spanish governor encouraged cultural assimilation among the sangleys who had converted to Christianity, and they were moved to Manila's Binondo area, now known as the oldest Chinatown in the world.

As Filipino-Canadian and University of Southern California associate professor Adrian De Leon writes in his 2016 essay '*Siopao* and Power: The Place of Pork Buns in Manila's Chinese History,' the Spanish vision of Chinese was one of entrepreneurs and capitalists, but they remained the perpetual 'other.'

'By the 19th century, the Chinese mestizo [descendents of sangley Chinese and native Filipinos, which included José Rizal] exerted influence on public affairs. The Spanish administration, seeing this as a threat, sought to turn the natives against the Chinese middle class to dispel anti-Spanish tensions,' De Leon writes. 'These attempts failed … By the end of the Spanish occupation, those with Chinese blood and those of native heritage were collectively known as "Filipinos" in the campaign for independence.'

In fact, author Luis H. Francia failed to mention the prevailing Chinese culture woven into the lives and dishes of Filipinos: lumpia are rice paper–wrapped spring rolls; *pancit*, the Philippine national noodle dish, means something 'quickly cooked' in Hokkien; while *siopao* literally translates to 'hot bun.'

Like Filipino food, the story of siopao, as Doreen Fernandez said, can be neither brief nor simple.

At family gatherings, after I'd spent hours sprawled on my tummy with my neck arched and my eyes dried from watching the television while we kids took turns playing Nintendo, a flash of hunger would jolt through me and I'd run downstairs. 'There's siopao,' my mom would say, as she pulled apart the plastic, hinged takeout container that housed six white buns.

She'd plop one onto a plastic plate and put it into the microwave for forty-five seconds. I'd watch that plate go round and round until she pulled it out and peeled off the square parchment paper at the base of the siopao (a trick that prevents the bun from sticking). Cutting it in half to reveal the shiny brown sauce and the quartered, salted duck egg inside, she'd hand me a Sprite and I'd march back upstairs. I could hardly wait until I had one free hand to take a bite.

Nicole Ponseca, author of *I Am a Filipino: And This Is How We Cook* and the restaurateur behind New York City's Jeepney and the now-closed Maharlika, one of Manhattan's first modern Filipino restaurants, says eating siopao is just like Kourtney Kardashian's famed 'Six Steps to Eating a Kit Kat' clip from *Keeping Up with the Kardashians* – everyone has a particular way they do it.

'My mother would rip the paper off the bottom, then gently peel the thin skin around the siopao, which is formed when steaming – it was a very thin, imperceptible crust,' Ponseca says. 'I adopted my mom's way of eating it, because you can sink your teeth into the gummy bread. The way people eat it shows me who *knows* siopao.'

This ubiquitous Filipino steamed dumpling, which one can find frozen in packs of six at any Filipino-run store in North America, is more than the sum of its parts – its Chinese-inherited bun, its meat filling with a Spanish name. One bun tells the story of our history as Filipinos – through conquest, commerce, and culture – and it will never be brief or simple. One thing is for sure: siopao is not just for kids.

Technically, It's a Ravioli

Kristen Arnett

Truth be told, what *isn't* a ravioli? If we're talking logistics, then a ravioli is an object that's simply comprised of two basic parts: an outer layer and a filled middle. Is the object required to be edible? Or does the meaning of ravioli expand further than that, to the kind of galaxy-brained thinking that would allow someone to claim that perhaps, just maybe, possibly, the skull itself is a ravioli?

Technically, yes.

Ravioli as dinner, sure, but what about ravioli as larger than that? Ravioli as a construct, ravioli as a concept. We should consider every opportunity for its growth and expansion. We can be thorough here. A mattress is technically a ravioli. So is a banana. Your girlfriend is a ravioli, if we're being

RAVIOLI

RAVIOLI

RAVIOLI

honest, and guess what, so is your mom. A four-door Toyota Camry, when it's carrying you and your friends out to a night at the bar, is, in fact, a ravioli. Cadbury Creme Eggs and Blow Pops? Sweetly delicious, cavity-inducing ravioli. The mosquito that buzzes around my head in the humid Florida night air, sucking my blood, is the most annoying ravioli yet. They circle me, those raviolis, pestering me with their questions, wanting me to label them. To inform them who they are. To announce them to the world. To give them a fixed place.

Technically, all I'm ever doing is naming ravioli.

There are plenty of people who would agree that the food pyramid is, of course, a ravioli. So, too, the bulb of the human brain lighting up as we pronounce each item, as we categorize and connect, as we eschew traditional modes of seeing for something more exciting, something infinitely more delicious.

But it wouldn't be the internet (also a ravioli) without the naysayers. Those who look at the magic we've wrought and pronounce it to be vulgar. They reply to my ponderings and make their own proclamations: that ravioli can be only one thing, and one thing alone, and that is the original product. To them, it's merely the pasta, the meat, the cheese. The OG exterior and its wholesome filling. They claim that saying anything else is an aberration. They refuse to see anything beyond the scope of their own narrow view.

Technically, Doubting Thomas was a ravioli.

But, I say, who among us hasn't changed from our original form? What isn't made better with age? Milk changes to cheese, which changes to aged parmesan, grated and dusted lightly overtop a steaming bowl of something good. If I can change, then so can my definition of myself, and so can our concepts of right and wrong. The pasta-bilities are infinite.

Technically, it's all ravioli.

Sink or Swim:
A Riff on the Essence
of the Matzo Ball

David Buchbinder

First, there is the texture: a properly created matzo ball, contained in its essential matrix of chicken soup, is a textural symphony, weaving sensory notes into a toothsome engagement with the ancestors, their demands, and their gifts. The fundamental tone is a slightly springy density that, upon meeting teeth, immediately releases, falling into porous pieces bursting with the golden broth. As the chewing continues, teeth, palate, and tongue work together to slice through and then press the tensile construction of the ball into releasing flavour bursts, which are made up of matzo, schmaltz (rendered chicken fat), eggs, salt, spices, and – in those versions worthy of consideration – a broth that is deep, rich, smoky, briny, and redolent of dill and carrot.

Of course, like all things Jewish – religious, cultural, political, or culinary – there are many versions of the matzo ball (MB), each with its tradition and each with its camp of profoundly partisan adherents who think their way is the true way, with the rest at best misguided and at worst dangerous fools. We will explore some of these variations in a moment, but let us first get the most common matzo ball controversy out of the way, the one that has been discussed ad nauseam in print and around almost every Jewish table.

Sink or swim?

Although that dichotomy sounds like it might be the container for yet another Jewish argument about the best survival strategy to meet current threats (e.g., Israel or the Diaspora, capitalism or socialism, anti-Semitism on the left or the right?), it is actually a deadly serious struggle over texture and consistency: is the essential MB light and fluffy or dense and chewy?

Like almost all culinary bifurcations (of which there are plenty in the Jewish world), the source of conviction seems to emanate directly from one's ancestral preference, which implies a generations-long membership in one camp or the other, though, of course, in these Enlightenment times, people have become freer to jump from one side to the other.

I will not mince words here: I align squarely with the swim side, with an important qualifier. For MBS to realize their full potential, they must be light enough to impart a feeling of freedom (the very essence of the Passover ritual is a celebration of freedom), porous enough to be fully infused with the contextual broth, and yet structured enough to provide robust resistance to the celebrant's incisors before yielding up their treasures.

It's worth mentioning that the very first Jewish cookbook in English, *The Jewish Manual* (published in 1846), comes down on the swim side: '[T]he paste [of ground matzo, suet, eggs, browned onion, spices, and salt] should be made into rather large balls, and care should be taken to make them *very light*.' (Emphasis added.)

The broth is the primordial environment in which the matzo balls can fulfill their potential, the primal plasma from which they are manifested.

MBS are powerful cultural signifiers, uniting Jews and our fellow travellers in a ritual, gustatory experience that provides a direct connection to a generations-long lineage. Like many other such signifiers in the Jewish landscape, MBS exist at the juncture of a halacha-mandated practice and centuries-old, folk-based food forms. (Halacha – literally 'the way of walking' – is usually translated as 'Jewish Law' and derived from the written and Oral Torah, and guides religious practices and beliefs as well as numerous aspects of day-to-day life.) Matzo is, of course, the unleavened 'bread of affliction' at the very core of the Seder, the Passover ritual meal. While at this point matzo and MBS are intimately linked in almost every way, matzo has a three-thousand-year history of incredible consistency in content and form, whereas MBS are both relatively recent in origin and surprisingly diverse in interpretation.

Matzo ball is the name given in English to the ritually charged bread dumpling originally called (in Yiddish) matzo kneydl, which shares an Old German root with the contemporary German word *knödel* (knot). It was also called matzo kloesse or, in Alsace, matzo knoepfle, though these have gone out of general usage. Nowadays, most Ashkenazi Jews, wherever found, use the Yiddish term, likely in its diminutive form of kneydlakh.

As boiled, unfilled bread dumplings with European roots, MBS share a lineage stretching back to Italy (the first known recipe is for a pheasant dumpling that appears in *Apicius*, a fifth-century Roman cookery text), spreading from there via Bohemia (where it was first called knödel) to the rest of Central and Eastern Europe. These early iterations tended to be made from stale, crumbled bread soaked in milk or water and mixed with fat, salt, and, sometimes, meat or cheese. It was really only with the advent of industrialized food processing that flour and meal became the base of almost all dumplings.

This is certainly the case with MBS. Matzo meal only came into being as a by-product of the early industrial manufacture of matzo, a process developed in the U.S. by the eponymous company that is still at the forefront of Ashkenazic ritual food: Manischewitz. But before he could invent matzo meal, Dov Behr Manischewitz (who actually wasn't a Manischewitz at all, but rather one Rabbi Abramson, a Lithuanian Jew who bought a dead man's passport and a new name in order to get out of Russia) had to create the first fully automated matzo-making factory in Cincinnati, Ohio. This innovation turned centuries of hand-matzo-making on its head, eventually transforming small-batch, basically round, and pleasingly irregular (and lumpy) flatbreads into the square, perforated, and fully predictable product we know today.

One of the central mysteries of matzo as we contemporary, industrialized Jews know it is how an essentially tasteless cracker fashioned out of nothing but (usually) white flour, salt, and water can be so compelling. The answer lies in the fact that its very blandness (with what, as some commentators insist, is a subtle nutty undertone) makes the matzo crackers a tabula rasa of taste, transformed by liberal applications of butter and salt.

Going further, it is the star ingredient in concoctions of eggs (matzo brei), chocolate and toffee (matzo crack), and a whole host of other memorable, celebratory treats. Some of the more recent forays into contemporary matzo-centric cuisine range from the culturally confused (matzo lasagne) to the gastronomically dubious (matzo-and-mustard-crusted chicken breast) to the realm of pure abomination (matzo truffles with Manischewitz glaze). The point that all these experimentalists refuse to recognize is that the pinnacle of matzo-based food art has already happened and has been rocking every Seder for at least the last two centuries: matzo ball soup.

But to arrive at MBS, we must first have matzo.

So what is it, and where did it come from? As mentioned above, it is a kind of flatbread positioned at the very centre of the Passover Seder ritual. In fact, the biblical name for this holiday is Chag HaMatzot (Holiday of the Matzos), not Pesach, which referred to the Paschal sacrifice, or Passover, which referred to the angel of death giving the enslaved Israelites a miss while dealing doom to sleeping Egyptian firstborn sons.

Matzo's essence is its unleavened (or unrisen) state, something that separates it from almost all other bread products the world over. This unleavened condition recalls the inability of the Israelites fleeing Pharaoh's wrath to wait long enough for their normal flatbread to rise. A quite surprising fact is that, according to Gil Marks in his magisterial *Encyclopedia of Jewish Food*, much matzo in pre-industrial cultures was often thick and soft, and this type can be found today in some Mizrachi (Middle Eastern) and Sephardic Jewish communities.

At first blush, industrial matzo seems to have little going for it as a food experience. For the uninitiated consumer, it has a blandness so complete that it cannot be said to have any taste at all. Add to this the fact that, when taken in its natural, unadorned state and chewed rigorously, matzo is quickly transformed into a pasty lump that, by its very desiccation (and the laws of diffusion), greedily sucks into itself all the moisture one's salivary glands can produce. But as the extracted saliva does its work, the danger of choking on the matzo-paste lump recedes and the mouth begins to restore balance to its ecosystem; the eater then notices a tasty impression emerging, hovering over the blandness like a Fata Morgana (mirage) in the desert.

A warm, if faint, nuttiness – the sweet promise of a full-blown taste treat – arises, awaiting some kind of alchemical process to unlock the flavour secrets of this benighted cracker. And that is where the matzo ball, inextricably linked to its companion, chicken broth, comes in.

My first MB memory takes place in my grandma Leona's kitchen on Ingleside Avenue in Baltimore, where she lived with her second husband, Nathan (who stepped into the breach after my grandfather Harry committed suicide), and her stepson Irv (who was about ten years older than me and the proud owner of the first *Playboy* magazine I ever saw). The white-shuttered brick house with a wide verandah was just down the block from the famed Pimlico Race Track.

I was four or five at the time and so it could not have happened during Pesach preparations. Why? We lived in St. Louis at the time and our Seders were always with a circle of St. Louis's left-wing Jewish activist families, among them the Madisons, the Gildens, and us. I didn't attend a Baltimore Seder until after we moved to Toronto when I was ten.

I'm pretty sure Grandma Leona was making MBS at my request, since few Jews of her generation routinely made this soup out of season. Also, it was Baltimore summertime: hot and humid out, warm enough for her to be wearing a light, smock-like summer dress with short sleeves and small pink flowers. I loved Grandma Leona – her Baltimore accent, her warmth, and her humour – until relatively early dementia took that humour and left her with one principal concern: whether any person she interacted with, none of whom she recognized, was married. It was a reasonable enough preoccupation for a woman of her generation and given form in her own life as she managed to bury three husbands. But I did not love that dress.

In any case, in this moment – what you might call my 'À la recherche du temps perJew' – Grandma Leona stands in her kitchen at her Formica table, her hands covered with MB preparation (made from scratch, of course), scooping it up and rolling dainty little spheres between her palms, her soft upper arms swaying in time. As each ball takes its form, she places it on a cookie sheet next to its compatriots – lined up and looking like a classroom of towheaded pupils – waiting to be popped into the pot.

The truth is, I don't have a specific memory of eating those MBs and their enveloping soup. The memory is all about me and Leona in her kitchen, just the two of us, her working – once in a while adding a bit of explanation of what she was doing – and me on a stool close by watching her and probably questioning her non-stop. I definitely had the feeling I was being initiated into some kind of mystery, as I did on other occasions when I watched her make chopped liver, but that's another story.

I do have a more generalized sensory imprint of Leona's chicken soup, which I would have eaten on many occasions in its un-MB'd form at Shabbos, Rosh Hashana, and other family gatherings. Not to speak ill of the dear departed, but I can say that this soup was, at best, satisfying: flavourful, if a bit salty and thin.

On the other hand, the soup of my mother, Judith (Leona's third child of four), started out strong and went from there, developing richness and complexity along the way as she continuously evolved her recipe. By the time I was a tween, she had perfected her art, as expressed in my opening salvo: 'deep, rich, smoky, briny, redolent with dill and carrot.' And of all the Jewish delicacies that fiery feminist and activist Judith would make (including her mother's chopped liver, which is still the only version I have ever liked), her soup sang to me the most – the delightful flavour derived from what I only discovered later was, in fact, the healing and nourishing properties of bones long simmered, the floral astringency of herbs, and the silkily satisfying mouth feel of fat. And her MBS took no back seat to her broth, fulfilling (and perhaps shaping) my personal requirements outlined above.

I had no sisters, and in any case the gendered segregation of food-preparation knowledge broke down across a time span fully consonant with my life so far. I became the bearer of our family soup continuum. For almost every year of our marriage, Roula Said, my Palestinian-Canadian wife, and I have hosted a very cross-cultural Seder full of Jews and our fellow travellers.

For every one of those Seders, I have been the maker of the soup and the kneydlakh. Over the decades, I have been involved in my own search for the most fulfilled expression of this cultural signifier. And, judging by the silence that usually greets the first slurps and bites of soup and knaidl, followed by vigorous expostulations of joy and approbation, I'm on the right track.

In the end, Jewish life, in its broadest sense, is incredibly rich and resilient, created out of an ancient, always evolving religious tradition and practice that is inextricably interwoven with an equally strong and evolving cultural tradition. Notwithstanding the existence of Israel, along with its political and cultural weight, Jews are still primarily a diasporic people who must, in every generation, renew our participation in Jewish life. It's a process that, all of the prophesies of assimilatory doom to the contrary, continues to happen even within mixed families like mine. An imperfect process, and yet it continues. The incredibly powerful and resilient rituals and the food create the form and content of this continuum.

A case in point: in the summer of 2021, our daughter Laila (one of the great kneydlakh lovers of all time) left home to move to Montreal to just work and live and to become a grown-up. She found herself a wonderful situation, with a Mile End apartment and three excellent roommates. When she told me that, for their Hanukkah party, they had collaborated on making matzo ball soup, my joy knew no bounds.

Solid, Glutinous, and Toothsome

André Alexis

A s a man born in the 1950s, in Trinidad, I've been acquainted with dumplings all my life. They aren't a defining aspect of who I am, but they occupy their own discreet and discrete place in my imagination. They don't mean any one thing to me. They aren't, for instance, an emblem of Trinidad, maybe because by the time I was aware of them as something other than an excellent part of split-pea soup, say, I was living in Canada, my parents having moved us there when I was three and a half.

I can't remember my first dumpling, but I remember an early and vivid sensation. I was almost certainly eating a soup of which they were part.[1] The dumplings were shaped like 'quenelles' of various sizes: that is, tapered at both ends and relatively thin. They were solid, glutinous, toothsome, tasting at first of the soup and then, after a first bite, of the flour, cornmeal, and salt from which they were made. They were somewhere between solid and airy, the culinary equivalent of a colloid, and the thisness and thatness of them was part of their pleasure. I mean, how lovely to bite into a thing, thinking it is a piece of potato or yam, only to realize, no, it's a dumpling.

It wasn't until much later that I ate Chinese dumplings, and I love them almost as much. But in my mind, the ur-dumpling, the dumpling outside of Plato's cave, is without filling, tapered, slightly salty, and a pleasant surprise in a soup.

Then, too, the thing about dumplings in split pea or cow heel soup[2] is that they thicken the broth. The feel of dumpling soup is rich, almost luxurious. In my memory, anyway, there are few things tastier. Of course, this is if you cook the dumplings with the soup, as opposed to cooking them separately and then adding them to the soup.[3]

The last time I ate dumplings – what *I* think of as dumplings, anyway – was in 2012, when I was living in Tobago, trying to write a novel.

The novel in question, of which I wrote a hundred pages, was set in Trinidad in the 1940s. In it, I described the childhood of a character named Henry Wing, who had figured in my first novel, *Childhood*. My mother and father both actively disliked the draft I showed them. Meaning: my father questioned whether the Trinidad I depicted was real, and my mother asked that her name be taken off the dedication page.

One of the points of contention was a passage I wrote describing the eating of monkey flesh. I'd had a long conversation with a young hunter, and he had described the process of hunting, skinning, and eating monkey. In the 1940s, monkey would have been considered wild meat, an expensive delicacy. My parents, however, denied that Trinis had ever eaten monkey and said that, whatever the case, I – who hadn't grown up there – did not have the right to criticize Trinidad, the place they were born.

I was born there, too – in a rooming house in St. Ann's, Port of Spain, where my mom's midwife lived. But I'd left it as a child, and my connection to the island is bound to an ever more vague sense of the place that I retain from my childhood.[4] So, tacitly agreeing with my parents, I abandoned the novel.

But to get back to the dumplings ...

The last dumplings I remember eating were in an iguana stew I bought in a restaurant in Buccoo, Tobago.

I'd had some of the cook's stews and soups previously. Her cow heel soup was tremendous. And once, while I was talking to her, she mentioned she would be making iguana. I'd never had iguana, but I wanted to try it, because ...

My host in Tobago, Joy Hackett, had told me how, one day, she happened on an iguana in the road, just after it had been hit by a car. She was quick to take it up. It was large, a real catch, she said. As it happened, the iguana had been hit just outside of someone's home. This person came out just after Joy and convinced her that she should leave the iguana with them, that they would take care of skinning and cutting it up, and then share it with her, half and half. When Joy went back to get her share, it had been cooked and eaten already.

Joy's disappointment at the memory of losing her share of iguana was palpable.

So, on the day the iguana stew with dumplings came out, I ordered some to go. Carrying the food back to the house, however, I just couldn't get the physical reality of iguanas out of my mind. For one thing, they're not prepossessing.[5]

For another, I once saw one get up on its hind legs and run, very quickly, across an empty lot. A disconcerting sight. And when it came time for me to taste the 'guana stew, I just couldn't bring myself to eat it. There was nothing untoward or strange-looking about the meat. It looked like chicken or pork, whitish beneath the sauce. But something stopped me from tasting it. Instead, I ate a piece of the dumpling included with the dish, then left the food for my roommate.

The moment I left the 'guana for my roommate was unexpectedly resonant. As a child, I'd always felt self-conscious about Trini food, *our* food.[6] That same self-consciousness returned when I was faced with the 'guana stew. Now, however, I was on the other side of a line: not Trini when faced with iguana, but Trini enough to go for the dumplings.

Belonging and not belonging, half this, half that: myself, my culture, colloidal.

NOTES

1. The first time I saw dumplings sitting beside a dish in a plate of their own, I had the feeling of something being 'off,' somehow. It was also odd seeing them circular, as I first did when I went back to Trinidad recently, or triangular, as they were when I was in Tobago.
2. Cow heel soup is, well, made with a cow's feet. More expansively, it's a split pea soup with dumplings, veggies, and the feet of a cow. It's also indescribably delicious when slow-cooked.
3. A note about coconut milk: though I feel almost un-Caribbean for saying so, I can't stand the taste of coconut milk in dumplings. I prefer regular milk, if you're using milk. This is a little odd to me, since I love the taste of coconut and coconut water. I suppose it has something to do with my expectations. When I'm eating pelau, for instance, I don't want to taste coconut. The only place I don't mind coconut milk is in callaloo. I blame my eccentricity, where coconut milk is concerned, on my emigration.

Though it's easy enough to find it these days, my parents didn't have ready access to coconut milk when we lived in Ottawa and Petrolia in the 1960s and 1970s. So I notice the presence of coconut milk in dumplings or pelau. And I dislike it.

4. Curiously, my more recent experiences of Trinidad and Tobago don't impinge deeply on the private and sensual version of the island that I retain from my earliest years.

5. I mean, they're not 'ugly' – whatever that word means – but I've never wondered what it would be like to sit beside one and watch TV, for instance.

6. My childhood notion of an 'exotic' and 'wonderful' food was mashed potatoes. At home, we generally had rice with our meals. I grew up around French-Canadians, however, and whenever I ate at a friend's home, I was always thrilled when the mashed potatoes came out. I was bewildered the first time I heard someone complain about having to eat mashed potatoes 'again.'

The Filling

Métis-Style Drop Dumpling Duck Soup

Miles Morrisseau

After living in Ontario for more than three decades, I went back to my maternal home of Grand Rapids, Manitoba, in 2019. My mom was having health problems, and if she was going to be at home, she needed support – the kind not easily accessible for people in northern communities. As a family, we all knew how important it was for Mom to be home.

She had moved away when she was still in her teens and soon met my father and began her own life. They had retired here around 2006, to the land owned by her father, grandfather, and great-grandfather, where she could sit out on the deck, drink tea, and watch the pelicans fishing on the Saskatchewan River. It was not just ancestral land – it was land our family had paid taxes on for as long as taxes have had to be paid in Canada.

I was the only one of my five siblings who did not have a regular job and who could also find ways of earning a living while helping my parents. My father is in phenomenal shape for a man in his eighties, but he had never been a caregiver, and there are some things an octogenarian can't learn.

Of all the things I had missed in those years I spent in Ontario, I missed my mom the most. She had all the goodness and faith that I needed. If she believed, I believed. She had the Cree language. She spoke and laughed in a special way – the way known so well by those of us who don't speak the language but grew up around it. It is the secret place. The special way of talking about and seeing the world.

I had been back for over a year, and my mother had made a significant recovery when it was revealed that her medication had not been properly managed after she had a cancerous tumour removed. Once her medication was adjusted, her concerning digestion and frightening fainting symptoms became a thing of the past.

Mom had always made duck soup just like she made the bread, the bannock, the rhubarb pie, and the deer meat stew.

On a fall day in the middle of a worldwide pandemic, my father cleaned the few fowl he'd caught, then singed them with an acetylene torch. The truth was they didn't look like much. But this was always the secret of duck soup – a little went a long way, and there would always be more broth than anything else. That was the point. It was the smoky, wild flavour of the duck meat and the rendered fat from a summer of feasting that provided the epicure's delight.

There is a debate around how much thickener should be added to the broth. Some people keep it thin while others add enough flour to give it a nearly gravy-like consistency. A few potatoes, salt and pepper, with just a little flour to add a consistency to the soup, is how my mom made it. She always served it with butter, fresh bannock, and Blue Ribbon Tea.

This time, however, *I* was making the soup.

I was born at St. Anthony's General Hospital in The Pas, Manitoba, in November 1964 and lived for the first winter of my life in an uninsulated cabin on the shores of Clearwater

Lake. It must have been one of the hardest winters in my parents' lives. I was their fourth child, and my father had recently left the army and moved with Mom and my older brother and sister from the Canadian Forces base in Edmonton back to my mother's home territory in Northern Manitoba. They were both twenty-five years old.

My father comes from a proud military tradition. He had three uncles who served during World War II, two of them on the front lines. Uncle Jim was captured in the Pacific theatre and suffered physical and psychological torture during the five years he spent in a Japanese POW camp. Uncle John stormed the beaches of Normandy as a member of the Royal Winnipeg Rifles, nicknamed the Little Black Devils. They blew past the German lines and had to be told to stop to wait for the Americans to catch up.

On one of the many long rides I took with my father when I returned home to help take care of Mom, he told me his dream had been to get an overseas deployment. And in the summer of 1964, he'd gotten a call from an old army buddy. They were deploying to Germany. All my dad had to do was re-enlist and he would be heading overseas, as he had long dreamed. But my older brother Marshall had already arrived since the family's return to Manitoba, and my mother was now pregnant with me. He could deploy, get settled in Germany, and send for the family. But didn't happen.

The smallest things. We grew radishes. They came in one of those strips you just push a half inch into the ground and cover up. I had filled up three fish boxes and put them on a low stand so my mom could garden without having to get down to the ground. The boxes had holes for draining, and I put stones and gravel in the bottom of them before filling the boxes up with a mixture of enriched soil from the store and natural soil from the ground.

The radishes popped up in a couple of days, and within a month they were ready to eat.

'Can you bring me some of those radishes with some butter on a plate?' my dad asked. I took a handful from our garden, rinsed off the dirt, snipped off the greens and the root tip, and put a dab of butter onto a plate. I brought it to my father. 'This is a real treat,' he said.

The radishes reminded me of sitting in the garden with my mom and eating them as a treat. My grandmother was a hardworking woman who prided herself on her garden and her cows. Eating her freshly churned butter with those freshly picked radishes – a true comfort food – was a special moment.

The fall is when hunting season begins. My parents, as Elders in the community, receive moose from the first hunt of the season, including a piece of the coveted backstrap. They also receive fresh pickerel fillets and succulent pickerel cheeks from local fishers. When my mother is not feeling well, she will put the word out, and soon enough a whitefish appears. In the fall and spring, my parents usually receive a goose and a couple of ducks. For some people, there is nothing better than a nice, fat fall duck, and my father is one of those people.

Grand Rapids and its sister community, the Misipawistik Cree Nation, sit on the south side of the Saskatchewan River, at one of the most important geographic points in Manitoba. Lake Winnipeg is the province's largest lake, and the river served as the highway for Indigenous Peoples since time immemorial and then for settlers for centuries.

The river allowed the residents to take a small boat and go into the smaller lakes, tributaries, and marshlands that make up the Saskatchewan River Delta. The river was the Trans-Canada Highway, the Route 66 of the North American continent's northwest. It gathers the water from the Rocky Mountains and carries all the water from all the connecting brooks, streams, and smaller rivers, then rushes it into the largest lake in Western Canada. The river dropped nearly twenty-five metres when entering the lake, creating the Grand Rapids, or what the Cree People called Misipawistik, the Singing Waters.

They say that after Manitoba Hydro dammed the river in 1964, some old people no longer felt like this was home, because the waters – which connect to the Churchill River system and the Arctic Ocean – had been silenced.

My father had gone out hunting with a friend who was at least fifteen years his junior and who complained of some non-specific ailment that prevented him from doing some of the most basic tasks that are part of boating and hunting. My father was never one to refuse any task or acknowledge that his octogenarian status meant he was an Elder who needed to be served. He had come up north the only way a poor Métis boy could back in the late 1950s: he followed the steel rails, swinging a spike hammer for an extra gang for the CN. There were no roads in those days.

When he got home with three fat ducks – he called them 'little butterballs' – he grumble-bragged about the things he had had to do for this younger friend. 'I had to jump in the water to pull the boat up onto the shore,' my dad told me. 'I had to knock all-a-dese.' Every now and then, my dad will slip into the southern Métis patois that is still strong in many communities. He says these places represent the Métis diaspora, although that is not a word he said or will ever say.

As my father relates the history of his own family, he tells the story of families right across the west. 'They were chased out of the "Postage Stamp,'" he would always say. The Métis people who brought Manitoba into Canada had lost their land and were forced to carve out new lives north, east, south, and west of their original settlement along the Red River, and on the original provincial territory they called the Postage Stamp.

The Morrisseaus, Moars, Ashams, Spences, and others all made homes along the shores of Lake Manitoba to create their own community in Crane River. Other families joined the community as the years passed. Many of those newcomers were women who had to leave the First Nation when they married non–First Nation men – who were almost always Métis – and lost their status rights. It was this way until 1985, when Bill C-31 was passed in the Canadian Parliament, eliminating gender discrimination.

Today, my uncle Louis, who is in his seventies, is the last of our line to live on land carved out by our ancestors over a century. That land is being taken away through the usual collaboration of government, business, and racism. The Métis couldn't buy land. My uncle was rich, but he could never buy an acre of land.

I knew my grandparents had money and that Granny was very savvy about earning it. She ran the taxi business that served both the Métis and First Nations side since many people needed rides to the closest town, Sainte Rose du Lac, where the nearest grocery store, bar, liquor store, bank, and restaurant were located.

I had heard the story many times about how Granny had taken full control of the family business when she bought her first cow – a cow that had been the last one in the yard and that my grandfather had traded away for the magic beans of alcohol.

From that one cow, she built a thriving ranch and taxi business, yet she couldn't buy the land under her feet. The land has since been gobbled up by outsiders, pension plans, and foreign investors; the settlers come in all colours and nations these days. My uncle has seen them all come and go over the last seven decades. It is hard work to make a life on these hard lands. And when he goes, the last of us will go with him.

I ran the family farm during the week from the time I was ten years old. It was just the way things were, and I didn't think about it until many years later. The farm was in Crane River, that Métis settlement with just over three hundred people on the swampy southwestern shores of Lake Winnipeg. It had a mercantile store and post office that was filled with lots of dusty merchandise that would never sell. It also carried tobacco, potato chips, chocolate bars, and RC Cola, the community choice. 'Coca-Cola is too sweet,' Uncle Leo would say.

Soon after settling in Crane River and building a barn with a stable, corrals, pigsties, and chicken coop, my dad started working in Winnipeg during the week. My oldest brother was already in Winnipeg attending high school, as the local school only went up to Grade 8. And my brother Marshall had lived with severe crippling arthritis from age one. He had plastic moulds made for his legs that he had to put on every night to keep the relentless disease from further twisting and wrenching his bones and joints. He moaned in pain all night long.

Three of us looked after the farm: Marshall, who rarely stayed in the house, no matter how hard the night may have been; our younger brother Monty, who was the baby boy of the family and knew how to get in and out of trouble; and me. We took care of the animals, and I handled most of the senior duties, including the driving.

All the animals had to be fed, cleaned, and bedded down at night. The cows had to be milked in the morning. I would boil water, then put it in the metal pail before I went out into the dark with a clean washcloth to prep the cows for milking. For the longest time, we had two cows. The black one was average size, with average udders, and as gentle as could be. It was not an exaggeration to say she was contented. The other one, however, was big and bullish, with long, thick teets that my boy hands could never quite pull completely. Her coat was off white, with flecks of red. Not contented, she hated to be milked. I always felt it was because we had taken her calf from her too early, and now we were stealing her milk after carting off her calf for sale. When the pail was almost full, she often kicked it over, and all that milk would go to waste.

I went to school in the provincial system, briefly in Grand Rapids and then The Pas and Winnipeg. Even though I spent only about a year in each stop, when I landed in the school in Crane River, I was already a year ahead of everyone else. So I skipped a grade in a school that went up to Grade 8. When I was twelve, I left for school in Winnipeg. I remember looking out the back window when we drove away and not understanding why my mom was crying.

For years, I had wanted to leave home. In spring 1981, when I was sixteen, my uncle Norman and my older cousin went to Winnipeg to collect my grandmother Lydia's body. Before the sun rose, they dropped me off at Union Station there. I sat on the platform, waiting for the CN office to open up, so

I could apply to work on a gang building railway sidings somewhere northwest of Armstrong, Ontario, near the open-pit amethyst mines. We would be given free passage and food vouchers.

If I was going to take this job, I had to take that train. I remember thinking that my grandma would have been proud – and my grandfather Stanley *was* proud. I knew then that my uncle Norman was also proud of me. But I didn't think a lot about what it meant to my mom, as people always take a mother's love for granted. As for my father's pride or respect, it was something I had long ago given up trying to achieve. The only thing that mattered to him was that I was working, and the only thing that mattered to me was that I was leaving.

It isn't hard making decisions. It's hard living with decisions. I didn't know how long I would be gone because no one ever knows which way we're headed when we make our choices at the crossroads, when we board those trains, when we choose that school or hold that hand.

It was like Mom says: 'You don't know God's plan for you until you are doing it.'

And I didn't realize how long I'd been gone until it had been far too long. At Uncle Norman's funeral in 2001, I was overwhelmed by how much I had missed and lost. Like his siblings and like my parents, Norman was the ultimate Métis person. He not only lived in both worlds but was master of each universe. He was successful in the white world and could also live off the land and the lake, with a balance that few could ever achieve.

I did not regret my decisions or the life I had made, but now I knew the cost. The people I grew up loving were going away, and many things had been left unsaid.

My life has been filled with love and laughter and food. So much food. My wife and I raised six kids and dozens of nephews, nieces, and cousins. We feasted the family seasonally, and I learned at the apron strings of my partner how to cook and fry and bake.

Under Mom's direction, I quarter the three birds and roll the dozen pieces in flour with some salt and a little too much pepper. The dredged pieces are browned in a tablespoon of Tenderflake lard in a heavy-bottomed soup pot, then water is added so the pot is about three-quarters full, with about three litres of liquid. It boils for an hour, or until the fat has rendered and gathers on top.

I add three medium-sized potatoes, and when those are cooked, the soup will be ready.

My father would not be offended if you called him a mama's boy. He loved his mother and was proud of the special relationship he had as the oldest son, her 'Sonny Boy.' He was proud that he left home at an early age, but it was his regret to have left his mother so soon.

As the smell of the duck soup begins to fill the room, my father reminisces about his mother's duck-soup dumplings. They didn't resemble the almost cake-like dumplings you often see on soups, he says; these were more like fat drops.

I call my auntie, who greets me with, 'Oh, Mack, how are you doing?' I tell her I am fine, and she asks how my parents are. She knows I have been up here for a bit. I ask how she is doing, and she goes on as moms do about her baby, and it is heartwarming. That kind of love is unconditional – one of the wonders of life. My cousin Julie is in her mid-forties, living with severe cerebral palsy from birth. She has never said a word, but there is no doubt that the love is returned.

The recipe is simple enough.

MÉTIS-STYLE DROP DUMPLINGS

1½ Tbsp lard
1 Tbsp baking powder
1¾ cups flour
¾ Tbsp sugar
½ Tbsp salt
1 cup milk

The trick, Auntie says, is the milk: 'You might need more, you might need less. You want a thick pancake batter.' Roughly a tablespoon at a time, drop the batter into the soup. Cover the pot.

When the soup is served, my dad is filled with a calm happiness.

My mom tries a few dumplings, but she is already breaking up her bannock and dropping the little chunks into the soup, the way she always does. Moms don't need anyone to make them feel at home.

Ask No Questions About Samosas

Angela Misri

The kitchen in my childhood home in Calgary was not a shared space. It was ruled by a maharanee who hated to be questioned. Unfortunately for her, she had sired a ridiculously curious child who not only questioned everything, but also cast doubt on recipes that had been passed down through generations, like a crazed toddler in a sweet shop.

That kitchen was the arena where I learned my mother's/ her mother's/her mother's mother's way of making pakoras and samosas.

The instruction would start in much the same way.

ANGIE: What are you making, Mom?

MOM: Pakoras. Go do your homework.

ANGIE: Why?

MOM: We have people coming over on Saturday.

ANGIE: Can I watch?

MOM: No.

ANGIE: Can I sit here?

MOM: (*Dramatic sigh, hands moving, mashing, folding, and then finally*) No questions.

My mom was the youngest child in a family of six siblings in Srinagar, Kashmir. Her only sister (my masi) was married at age fourteen when my mom was five or six, which meant she grew up as the focus of the feminine energy of *her* mother – the only person in the household to pass on the feminine arts. My nani was in a hurry. Mom had to be married off at sixteen because her mother was a widow. My nani was terrified that she would die and leave her young daughter at the mercy of her brothers (a weird logic, if you ask me, since she instead handed her daughter to a family she barely knew).

I bring up this family dynamic because I can't imagine that my nani's kitchen was anywhere near as adversarial as my mother's, both because my mother actually gets along with people and questions little, but also because when it came to preparing my mother for her future, my nani knew of two important things to pass on: cooking and caring for children. My mom had been raised to understand that not only was the kitchen her place, but it was her queendom. This was not to be the case for many frustrating years.

My mother went from her mother's kitchen, where she learned by watching (and supposedly not asking questions), to her sister-in-law's kitchen, where she was barred from entry as the youngest (and therefore lowest-ranking) wife in the Misri household, my father's family. Those were hard years for my mom, and not just in the kitchen. When she and my dad moved from his brother's home in Delhi to London, England, in the 1970s, she reclaimed her rightful place as the maharanee of her kila. Looking back, I understand why she put up some serious battlements.

In my mind, my mom's attempts to turn my attention back to my homework had two motivating factors: to focus me on the future she foresaw for me as a financially independent woman who lived in Canada, and to get me to stop badgering her with questions she didn't know the answers to, or didn't want to think about.

ANGIE: What's that?
MOM: Zeera. (*Sprinkles the small, dark, seed-like spice onto the mashed potatoes already in the bowl*)
ANGIE: What's that?
MOM: I told you – ZEERA.
ANGIE: (*Expert eye-rolling and as much teenage attitude as is wise this close to the wooden spoons*) No, what's the ENGLISH name of it?
MOM: Why does that matter? (*Ramping up to exasperated, hands moving faster to try to end this conversation sooner*)
ANGIE: How will I find it in the grocery store if I ask for zeera?
MOM: (*Dramatic sigh, scooping spices back into the cupboard like I've insulted them*) No questions.

This was one of the key arguments my mother and I had when making any kind of Indian food: she saw my demands for the translation of Indian spices into sometimes entirely different English names as a form of colonialism (though she never said that word), while I saw her intransigence as a way to keep secrets from me.

My mom shopped in the northeast end of Calgary for her spices. In those stores, she didn't need to think about English names for anything; the sealed bags were, in fact, labelled with their Hindi names because they had been imported from India, like zeera (black cumin), ajwain (carom powder), and haldi (turmeric powder). She even bought special rolling pins and bowls from these stores. To my teenage eyes, these implements looked archaic. I sense now that they reminded her of the simplicity of her own mother's kitchen back in Kashmir. But as the daughter of immigrants, I was determined to take advantage of all the variety that the 'regular' grocery stores afforded, so I was constantly trying to drag her toward what I saw as the future.

ANGIE: Mom, we should buy this!

MOM: What is this?

ANGIE: It's called phyllo. I found it in the frozen section.

MOM: Put it back.

ANGIE: But it looks just like a samosa. Look at this picture. Doesn't it look like a samosa?

MOM: We don't need it.

ANGIE: But the samosa dough takes forever! Look, with this we can just make the potato and pop it into this dough! Can we try it?

MOM: No.

ANGIE: Why? Maybe I could make samosas too, then? Maybe we could have samosas when people *aren't* coming over.

MOM: (*Dramatic sigh, throws the package into the shopping cart*) Go get some milk.

Suffice it to say that the phyllo experiment did not work. But I'm not convinced it was the frozen pastry's fault. My mother had a way of passive-aggressively using my curiosity about food to teach me lessons about this Western society I was so madly in love with. In my household, we ate Indian food almost every night, so I desperately craved the Canadian food I saw in TV commercials and my friend's lunch boxes at school. I went to Girl Guide camp at some point and fell in love with Hamburger Helper, of all things. When I came home, I begged my mom to buy it for us. After a conversation much like the one about phyllo, she relented. She made it for us that night and served it to my sister and me while she and Dad ate their usual vegetable and rice dinner.

ANGIE: (*Poking at the radioactive, orange-coloured stuff in the bowl*) This doesn't look right.
MOM: I followed the instructions on the box.
ANGIE: There's no meat in it!
MOM: I don't cook beef, you know that!
ANGIE: It's called Hamburger HELPER. It helps the hamburger. Without the hamburger, it's …
MOM: You wanted it. You eat it.

At some point my sister escaped this punishment, choosing no dinner over the concoction in front of her (fair, I guess, since I brought it upon us). But I had to eat a whole serving of Hamburger Helper pasta without the hamburger. Just so you know, the spices are in a pre-measured packet meant to be poured into a pound of meat. Without the meat, you are basically eating an extreme amount of salt and MSG on a little pasta. I was sick for at least the weekend, and I never asked for Hamburger Helper again. My mother is an exceptional cook of Indian food, even Indian foods she didn't grow up with. This was not a mistake. It was her way of teaching me that the Canadian culture I valued above her Indian one had its good points, but Hamburger Helper is not one of them.

ANGIE: (*Mashing potatoes with a fork*) Can we get an actual potato masher?

MOM: What for?

ANGIE: (*Points at the bowl in front of her*) This would go way faster with a masher.

MOM: (*Takes the fork and the bowl, mashes the whole thing quickly and expertly, hands it back with triumph mixed in*)

ANGIE: I still think a masher would be better.

MOM: Go do your homework.

The fact that I managed to absorb the way my mother makes pakoras and samosas at all is a minor miracle. If you asked her to write down 'the recipe' (and I have done this), so much of the direction would be 'as much as needed' or 'until ready.' I don't know why my mother balked so hard against solid recipes with consistent bullet points and instructions. She never (to my knowledge) used them herself. But her non-Indian cooking suffered from her determination to recreate with just her mind and instincts. We, the recipients of these rare Canadian dishes, suffered the most.

My mom always felt that being married so young limited her potential to be financially independent – a problem she was determined to solve for her two daughters, with complete success. I have to think that part of her reticence in involving us in the kitchen work was pushback against what she had been burdened with and denied. Her mother, my nani, had made her into a homemaker. Mom wanted more for her daughters. So she had all the time in the world for us and our traditional education. But she had much less time and patience for passing on the family cooking skills.

ANGIE: How big do you need to roll those circles? (*Squinting into the Facetime video call*)

MOM: This big. I'm showing you. (*Points to the perfectly symmetrical circles of dough rolled out in front of her*)

ANGIE: Mom, we're on Facetime, I can't tell how big they are.

MOM: Here. (*Demonstrates the rolling-out procedure again, producing a ninth perfect circle on her counter*)

ANGIE: Like, the size of your hand or the size of a dinner plate?

MOM: I'll just make them. Tell me how many you need.

ANGIE: No! I want to learn.

MOM: Then watch! This is how I learned. I didn't ask questions. I just watched. I learned.

Thus endeth all lessons.

VEGGIE SAMOSAS

POTATO FILLING
4 potatoes
¼ cup green peas
Pinch of asafetida (heeng)
½ tsp salt (namak)
1 Tbsp oil (or melted ghee)
1 Tbsp grated ginger
2 chopped green finger chilis
1 tsp ground coriander (dhaniya)

½ tsp red chili powder (mirch)
½ tsp fennel powder (saunph)

DOUGH
2 cups all-purpose flour
¾ tsp salt (namak)
¼ cup oil (or melted ghee)
¾ tsp carom seeds (ajwain)
About 6 Tbsp of water

1. Preheat the oven to 400°F and set aside two baking trays and parchment paper.

2. In a big bowl, add all the dough ingredients, except the water, and mix well with your hands or a mixer. You want the dough to hold its shape. Add a spoon of water at a time and work it in – you are trying to create a dough that is more stiff than soft. Cover with a towel and set aside for 20 minutes.

3. While the dough is resting, peel the potatoes, chop them into fours, then boil till just soft (not mashed-potatoes soft – just before). Then mash them in a bowl.

4. Heat a pan with a bit of oil or ghee (1 Tbsp) and cook up the cumin seeds over low heat (do not burn – start over if they burn). When they are golden, add the grated ginger and fry for about 30 seconds. Add the green peas and sauté for a couple minutes.

5. Add the red chili powder (the ½ tsp is a conservative amount) and the fennel powder, and sauté for 30 seconds before adding the potatoes and sautéing for 2 to 3 minutes on low heat. This is the opportunity to taste the mixture. You're going to be wrapping it in dough, so if you don't

taste the salt or red chilis now, you should add some (a ½ tsp at a time) because the dough dilutes the taste of the salt and spices.

6. Pop the dough out of its bowl onto a floured counter and start kneading. Make five smaller balls out of your original larger ball. Put four of the balls back into the bowl, cover them, and focus on one ball at a time on the counter.

7. Roll this one ball into a circle/oval the size of a dinner plate about half a centimetre thick. You should not be able to see your countertop through the rolled-out dough. Cut this rolled-out circle of dough into two halves (this will make two samosas).

8. Put a spoonful of the potato/pea mixture into the centres of both half circles, and then, along all the edges of the two half circles, apply water with your finger to make them a little sticky. Then fold them into the conical/ triangle shape of a samosa, pressing along the slightly wet edges to make them stick. At this point, you will find out if you added too much potato/pea mixture or if you made the dough too skinny. Adjust both as you see fit. I sometimes press down the edges of the samosa with a fork just to doubly seal them.

9. Place the samosas on the parchment-lined baking trays as you make them, spaced apart so they do not touch each other.

10. Before you pop them in the oven, lightly brush them with a bit of melted ghee or oil and then bake them for 15 to 20 minutes or until golden brown.

ONION PAKORAS

ONION FILLING
2 medium yellow onions
1 tsp chopped green chilis
¼ tsp turmeric powder
½ tsp garam masala
1 Tbsp carom seeds (ajwaim)
½ tsp asafetida (heeng)
½ tsp salt

DOUGH
1 cup chickpea flour
Water
Sunflower oil

1. Chop onions finely and add to a bowl with the chopped green chilis and all the spices, then mix well with a fork.
2. Put the bowl aside for a half-hour to let the water leach out of the onions (so you will know how much water to add and it won't be too much).
3. Add the chickpea flour and mix. You want this mixture to be thicker than cake batter, and you're going to drop spoon-sized clumps of it into hot oil, so you want it to hold together.
4. I tend to taste it at this point for both spice and salt – add more of each if you can't taste them (the batter tends to mellow everything).

You have a couple of options for cooking them, but, in either case, use a large spoon or a small ladle to measure out the pakora batter:

1. If you want to bake them, set the oven to 400°F, lay out a baking pan with a layer of parchment paper, and bake for 20 minutes.
2. If you want to fry them, warm up the oil in a deep pan till it's hot but not bubbling/boiling, then drop in the batter from just above the oil. You will need to flip them in the oil to get them golden and put them on a paper towel before serving.
3. I've heard that you can also air-fry them, but I've never done this myself.

Note: You can add almost any vegetable to the batter of the pakora (cauliflower, zucchini, potatoes) – just keep the pieces small.

A Spicy Labour of Love

Perry King

Even though I grew up with a small kitchen in a small Parkdale apartment in Toronto, I was exposed to a lot of flavours and textures. My parents, Guyanese to the bone, made the most of that space, concocting dishes swimming with flavour – evoking holiday dinners and family get-togethers in Georgetown.

Those memories shine for me as I try to emulate and develop dishes of my parents' homeland, from the sweet to the spicy. My mom, tall in stature and with a delicate hand, dredged up so much good food in that Parkdale kitchen.

The best part of Mom's chicken and vegetable soups – complex, delicious bowls of heaven – were the dumplings. They were the exclamation point made at the end of a labour of love – an hours-long effort to develop soups that were flavourful, spicy, and dense with nutrient-rich vegetables like squash, plantain, and spinach.

The broth – peppery, fruit scented, and savoury on the palate – would be delightfully spicy and welcoming. It was a dish she would share at large feasts with friends and family.

I remember the first time I tasted that soup, pepper sauce included. Mom had delivered a soup so potent that it made my eyes water. I was eight years old, and her soup was made from scratch. It was overwhelming – all I can remember is that it made me immediately uncomfortable and sweaty.

The kitchen would always smell spicy, and I was initially afraid of spicy sauces and foods. But, while my adjustment to spicy Scotch bonnet peppers would take many years, those mild, finger-shaped dumplings were a relief – and, honestly, would be the first thing I finished whenever she made her soup. Embracing them has opened up my taste buds and helped me make more solidified cultural connections to Guyana and its beautiful cuisine.

After hours of simmering the broth, my mom dropped the dumplings into the pot and let them cook for mere minutes. But first, she would roll them into small slender logs using just flour, baking powder, and salt mixed with water or milk. Making them was simple enough, but these dumplings provided a fatty and textural punch that complemented and tied together all the soup ingredients.

Caribbean soup dumplings have origins that date back to the nineteenth century, with a heavy influence from Chinese immigrants who arrived as indentured workers to Jamaica, Trinidad, Cuba, and Guyana – perennially sugar-producing islands. With scarce resources available to the indentured, families would make even dumplings with cassava root – a tradition that continues to the present day.

Preferences for soup dumpling ingredients differ drastically among Caribbean folks – whether you are adding (or not adding) spices, milk, or baking soda for basic dumplings in Jamaica and Guyana or making a more sophisticated, labour-intensive stuffed dumpling in Trinidad. Regardless, I share with you a general dumpling recipe that could fit with any of them and simmer its way into your heart and belly.

CARRIBEAN SOUP DUMPLINGS

INGREDIENTS
¾ cup flour
½ tsp baking powder
½ tsp salt
¼ tsp black pepper
¼ cup milk (can be substituted with warm water)

METHOD
Combine all dry ingredients before adding the milk (or water). My mom and I definitely recommend shaping the batter into finger-like forms, but take care not to make the pieces too big for this recipe. The batter should fall off the spoon easily when you're forming shapes.

When dropping the dumplings into the simmering broth, make sure to stir the soup, as this helps get the cooking process started, helps the dumplings absorb the broth flavour, and discourages the dumplings from sticking together. They will cook in approximately 5 minutes, but they can simmer for 15 minutes.

Tip: Sometimes, Mom and I keep baking powder out of the recipe to prevent the dumplings from expanding too much in the broth. Trial and error will help determine how much you include and if you need it in your batter at all.

VARIATIONS
You can add spices, like cayenne or cumin, for a deepened flavour profile, but ideally your soup is already spiced enough that adding more seasoning to the dumpling batter is

unnecessary. Still, you can certainly experiment with your dumpling combinations.

Herb Dumplings: Add a tablespoon of finely chopped parsley or any other herbs to your dry ingredients.

Carrot Dumplings: Add ⅓ cup of diced carrots to your dry ingredients.

Cheese Dumplings: Add ¼ cup of grated cheese to the dry ingredients. You can use any cheese but try to select one that balances the taste and texture of the soup – e.g., cheddar – whose flavour is not all that overwhelming.

Corn Dumplings: Substitute cornmeal for the flour. Absolutely delicious!

The Dumpling in Me Honours the Dumpling in You

Sylvia Putz

I discovered Asian dumplings thirty-five years ago, when I first moved to Toronto. Doused in soy sauce and sprinkled with something spicy, they were a lip-smacking revelation of shapes, sizes, textures, and flavours. I never imagined actually trying to make them.

The closest I'd come was watching the deft movements of women making dumplings in the windows of Chinese restaurants. But one cold evening in the fall of 2021, the dumpling ladies were us – a group of neighbourhood women of a certain age who normally wine and nibble as part of our monthly book club. We are a diverse group, ranging widely in ethnicity, marital status, profession, and in our literary preferences. But one thing is for certain – we take pleasure in each other's company.

After our last gathering, I had suggested over the din that we meet for a cookie exchange before Christmas. Lucy said, 'Pfft! How about a Korean dumpling-making party?'

For once, we all agreed.

Lucy was born in Korea and came to Canada with her family as a child. She's now a glamorous real estate agent with a cute black Volkswagen Beetle, a solid tennis game, and a Zen outlook. She arrives in her black puffer coat, carrying a bowl of filling. A large cloth bag hangs from her elbow.

Christine arrives next, bundled in a tweedy wool coat and a long mustard scarf, bearing a large stainless-steel bowl covered in plastic wrap. She is old-stock Anglo, not the hugging type, but politely endures my attempt. She manages a science lab and is detail oriented. I know she'll be supremely efficient at dumpling making.

The rest of the gang follow, all similarly loaded down – Erika and Emilia and, finally, Bernie.

Bernie takes off her coat, smooths back strands of her dark wavy hair, and adjusts her glasses. She is a bookkeeper and likes to do things precisely and perfectly, including her crowd-pleasing gourmet dinners.

'Remember your delicious Filipino rolls?' I ask. 'What are they called – lumpies?'

She laughs. 'Lumpias, not lumpies.'

The group ambles into my kitchen, chattering like happy sparrows.

'Did I hear something about lumpias?' asks my husband, who gets up from his computer. His family emigrated from India when he was seven and regularly had large multicultural and multigenerational parties that featured a huge pile of delicious lumpias made by a Filipina friend.

'No lumpias, but plenty of dumplings!' says Bernie.

'Lucy is the expert. She'll be whipping our butts if we don't follow her directions exactly!' I say.

'You better believe it,' Lucy replies. 'I'll make sure the production line keeps moving!'

My son, a university student, pokes his head shyly around the corner. 'Hi,' he says.

Lucy looks at him. 'Wow, are you ever tall!'

She walks over to him and looks up. 'It's good to be tall. Look at me – I'm so short, I can't see above people's heads at concerts.' She lowers her voice. 'What do they feed you?'

He smiles. 'Not enough dumplings. Call me when they're ready,' he says as he goes down to the basement.

Lucy makes a beeline to our dining table and lays out all her supplies.

Lucy is the only one in our club to have selected a self-help book as her pick. The rest of us chose memoirs or fiction. She introduced us to the notion of namaste, a respectful message of gratitude or greeting used often in yoga practice. The word, she explains, means 'the light in me honours the light in you.' I like the idea of it, the recognition that we all have a spark of the divine inside us.

My personal divinity, unfortunately, doesn't extend to the fine-fingered folding of delicacies, especially compared to the other fabulous cooks in the group. I've often written about my eating experiences but did not necessarily get involved in the actual cooking part.

A few days earlier, Lucy had sent us all an email, instructing us to bring our own wonton wrappers. Most of us ended up with frozen wrappers – only Erika managed to find the more delicate fresh ones. And I couldn't find kimchee – out of stock – so I begged Lucy for some; she always seems to have tubs of the spicy, fermented cabbage, a Korean staple, at her house.

A day later, she sent out further instructions to bring a baking sheet for finished dumplings and a supply of zip-lock bags. I started worrying, imagining that everybody's dumplings would end up crammed into my already-overfilled freezer.

Lucy laughed at me. 'Do you really think we'd leave all our dumplings in your freezer? They'd be eaten!'

'You've got a point,' I replied. My husband and son were ecstatic about the idea of having dozens of dumplings in the freezer, ready for plopping into a pot of boiling water for late-night snacking, and I didn't disagree.

Lucy explained to me that we must form the dumplings, boil them, and oil them at my house. Then they can be packaged and taken home to freeze. And we'll be frying a few for tasting before they go home.

'Ah,' I said, comprehending at last.

The ladies pack themselves, elbow to elbow, around the table. It's crammed with bowls, baking sheets, wonton wrappers, zip-lock bags, and even a pierogi-maker from Erika that we try and then discard.

'Did you get my email about how to fold a dumpling?' Erika asks. For years, she's been hosting foreign students who seek her out for her excellent cooking and her grasp of the intricacies of international cuisine. If anybody can make the perfect dumpling, it's Erika.

'I'll be lucky if mine stick together at all,' replies Emilia. She is new to the group, a former teacher who moved onto our street after she retired. 'I've made ravioli – my mother taught me how to make them. I used to hate it.'

'It's all worth it in the end,' says Lucy.

I recall that my mother didn't enjoy making semmel-knoedel from scratch either. She preferred making them from a package she picked up at the German deli in Guelph. I think she was turned off by the idea of mucking about in a bowl of bread cubes soaked in milk with onion, butter, eggs, spices, and, always, chunks of bacon. They were nothing like Korean dumplings, but they were carb heaven to me, served with lots of gravy.

Lucy had emailed everyone her mother's traditional Korean pork-and-beef dumpling recipe. Christine and Bernie faithfully reproduced the filling, Emilia decided on mushroom, and Erika brought a chicken-and-pork recipe.

'I settled on shrimp,' I say. 'And a tofu-and-kimchee recipe.'

Lucy frowns. 'We're meat eaters mostly. Never had a vegetarian dumpling.'

'I like kimchee, and pickled stuff in general,' I say. 'I inherited it from my German dad with his Baltic background. Anything fishy or salty.'

'Maybe you do have some Korean background,' says Lucy. 'But I doubt it.'

'Yeah, my butt is a little too big to be Korean,' I admit.

The women laugh.

I select Korean pop music on Spotify. Lucy shoots me a look as I take a seat between Christine and Bernie.

Christine is a shockingly fast dumpling maker. I am still getting settled while she produces dozens of dumplings that sit smugly on her baking sheet.

My husband volunteers to be the boiler. He dons his apron and stations himself at the stove with a large pot of water. He turns up the heat.

We seal our dumpling pouches with drips of water. I use square wonton wrappers, folding them diagonally into fat and leaky triangles.

'Just one teaspoon of filling,' Lucy says. 'That's enough.'

I follow her directions and start to produce competent dumplings that stick together but still look a little mushy.

'Only a few drips of water,' she cautions.

I steal glances at Christine's neat pile and Bernie's restaurant-perfect versions, consistently shaped and filled to just the right amount.

Erika's beautifully constructed dumplings are astounding. She may have even practised at home – I wouldn't put it past her. Her dumplings are beautifully formed, with dainty scalloped edges and little puckered bellies.

Emilia uses round wrappers to produce perfectly semicircular and well-padded dumplings chock full of her savoury mushroom stuffing.

My dumplings, however, look like elongated manta rays stranded on baking-sheet beaches. I catch dubious glances from the women but decide to ignore them. I tell myself these are shrimp dumplings, meant to look like they came from the sea.

Lucy darts around, playing the role of instructor and fixer. 'Handle the wrappers more delicately when you pinch them shut,' she says. 'Don't stretch them.' She mixes together white vinegar and soy sauce for dipping. She effortlessly produces perfect pork-and-beef dumplings between her bouts of helping.

Now the trips to the boiling station start in earnest. With a slotted spoon, my husband gently lowers the dumplings into the bubbling water, where they simmer until they rise to the top. He skims them off and hands them to the proud dumpling maker, who offers everyone a sample, lubricated with Lucy's dipping sauce.

The dumpling-making slows down every few minutes as we test the samples. Bernie's are insanely delicious! Christine's are just as tasty. Erika's are fantastic! Lucy fries a few so we can slurp these lovely, oiled, browned, and crispy dumplings down our gullets.

I hold my breath as my husband slides my dumplings into the boiling pot. I expect them to fall apart and spill their guts into the bubbling water. But they hang together, sinking slowly to the bottom of the pot. After a few minutes, they float serenely to the top, still intact.

Nervously, I offer up my shrimp dumplings to the women. They chew thoughtfully. Their eyes meet mine. 'So good,' they say.

I allow myself to taste one. Absolutely yummy! I pump my arm in triumph.

We taste Emilia's last. They're savoury, hearty, subtly spiced, and have the pleasing umami of cooked mushroom. Lucy thinks they do not taste like Korean dumplings. I can imagine them swimming in a buttery sauce, flecked with Italian parsley.

We finish boiling, then lovingly massage oil into our dumplings, so they can be slipped into zip-lock bags to take home.

Christine says she has to leave to go to yoga. I say, 'Namaste,' and bow slightly, hands pressed together in front of my chest.

One by one, the others gather up their dumplings and their supplies and head home. I realize there had been no wine drinking or raucous stories, as we normally have at book club. We'd been too busy. And I still hadn't finished my tofu-and-kimchee dumplings!

Lucy takes pity on me and stays to help. We finish them, pronounce them to be pretty good, with the sharp taste of kimchee and the heartiness of marinated tofu. But she still prefers her mother's traditional meat recipe, she says. Into the freezer they go.

Lucy elbows me. 'Call your son.'

Soon I hear the thumping of feet up the basement stairs. He sniffs appreciatively.

Lucy pulls out her bag of dumplings and tips them into the pot of hot water.

He stops, shocked. 'Those are your dumplings – I don't want to eat yours. What will you take home?'

'Oh, I've got plenty at home,' Lucy replies. 'Believe me.'

His eyes are glued to Lucy and the dumplings. She finally slips a huge pile of golden and well-oiled dumplings onto his plate and watches with obvious pleasure as he – there is no other suitable word – vacuums them up.

As we clean up, Lucy tells me I am 'pure in spirit.'

'Oh, thank God, Lucy. I wouldn't want to be impure.'

She tsks. 'What I'm saying is that you're like a dumpling. A little soft in the middle, maybe also in the head, but beautiful and full of good ingredients.'

'Well,' I say, 'I sound absolutely delicious. Nobody could resist me.'

Lucy slips on her coat, and I give her a hug.

'So very nice to have people like you in my life,' I say.

As she heads out into the night, I feel blessed to live in a community of friends, all different in so many ways, who enjoy each other's company, read books, share opinions, drink wine, and, now, make Korean dumplings together. What could possibly be better?

On Modaks:
Offerings of Little Bliss

Mekhala Chaubal

It catches my eye at the same moment as it captures the sparkle of the setting sun: the little silver dumpling, a squat offering to the matching idol of Ganapati in the newly set-up shrine in our new-to us home in Hamilton, Ontario. It is August 2021, and we have just moved in. I look over the rest of the personal family pantheon of deities before me – with countless gods and goddesses to choose from, it certainly helps to have a few personal favourites.

As a child visiting my grandparents in Pune, India, I was introduced to Ganapati (or Ganesha) more as a friend than a god – a trunk-swinging, single-tusked, elephant-headed deity, traversing the confines of space and time on a bandicoot rat (a demon cursed into this form for eternity). Ganapati searches for universal knowledge, has a penchant for sweet coconut dumplings (more on that later), and removes obstacles. He is one of the most important gods of Hindu Maharashtrians, who live in the state in western India from which my family claims its heritage.

This description is an oversimplification, of course. Ganapati is also worshipped as the patron deity of scholars, intellectuals, and, aptly, writers. Indeed, my countless panicked utterances before anxiety-inducing school exams were invariably directed toward him as the keeper of all wisdom and knowledge – of both the divine and more earthly kind.

With such a loaded portfolio, it's only natural to feel a bit peckish, you might say, and Ganapati seemingly agrees. His food of choice, the breakfast of this champion, is a humble, coconut-and-jaggery-stuffed, cardamom-infused steamed rice dumpling called a modak, loosely translated as 'a piece of bliss.'

One myth tells of a time when little Ganapati, being served a feast at the home of the revered sage Atri Rishi, just couldn't get enough of anything. His voracious appetite left his parents, Lord Shiva (he of the Hindu trinity as the Destroyer) and the Goddess Parvati (she of the manifestation of Shakti, the feminine force of the universe), and the rest of the ashram starving. So, Anasuya – Atri's wife, and the chef par excellence in this story – finally handed him a modak, which little Ganapati promptly scarfed. To his delight, and everyone else's, he declared his hunger to be sated. The parallel between spiritual and real hunger is obvious, and so the modak has come to symbolize the bliss of finding transcendent knowledge, one delicious mouthful at a time.

But how do we know, as mere mortals, what the perfect number of modaks are when offering them at Ganesh Chaturthi, the annual festival dedicated to Ganapati? Twenty-one seems to be the agreed-upon number. The reason has to do with the twenty-one burps released by Shiva at the aforementioned modak feast of Anasuya. Still, though, how do we really know that twenty-one modaks will be enough?

'It's a feeling,' says my grandma. 'Wouldn't twenty-one modaks fill *you* up? Think about it.'

In my memory, eight-year-old me is giggling with delight at the thought of my hands and freshly sprouted trunk inhaling modaks in twos and threes. Happiness. Bliss. Ecstasy. Call it what you will – it's a feeling I've learned to associate with Ganapati, with the joy of learning something, and, in a way, with my own personal understanding of faith.

Which is why, as I look at the kernel of silver pastry before Ganapati as I arrange the shrine in our dining room, I think about the sudden loss of my grandma to COVID-19 a few months earlier, and the fact that I haven't felt anything remotely faithful since. In that moment, I know I have a new mission. 'I'm making modaks tonight,' I announce to no one in particular.

It's the middle of a heat wave in July, months before the beginning of Ganesh Chaturthi, and I can't explain this sudden, unshakable urge. My ever-patient wife tags along for the ride, fingers woven through yarn, knitting in time to the chatter of my cooking plans. We traverse the streets of Hamilton, still unfamiliar after a recent move from Toronto, and find that the ingredients are thankfully available at a nearby Indian grocery store. Returning home, I lay out the simple ingredients on the kitchen counter almost reverentially –

jaggery, ghee, thawing coconut flakes, rice flour, cardamom, and nutmeg. It's showtime.

Ukadicha modak – the steamed version I'm trying out – has a reputation for seeming simple until you actually attempt it. Or perhaps we Maharashtrians are just not a dumpling people, per se. Funnily enough, apart from modaks, they don't feature prominently in our cuisine anywhere else. Whatever the reason, the actual making of these dumplings is, for me, shrouded in mystery. When she prepared them, Grandma simply shooed us out of the kitchen, only to present us with steamed perfection a few hours later. Now it's my mother to whom I turn for advice, as she is the keeper of the matriarchal, modak-making wisdom.

'What comes first?' I ask. 'The dough or the filling?' The latter is a concentrated mix of jaggery, ghee, shredded coconut flakes, cardamom, and nutmeg – at least in our family's version of the recipe.

'You're a good-news-now kind of person,' she replies. 'Do the filling.'

I can't argue with that logic.

Ganesh Chaturthi is not a quiet festival. In my family's state of Maharashtra, it is a five- to ten-day-long affair, complete with private and public fasting, feasting, and communal evening rituals before either family or public idols of Ganapati. The celebration marks the arrival of the little elephant-headed god and his mother, Parvati, at Mount Kailash ('crystal' in Sanskrit), the family home of the Shiva-Parvati clan. Ganapati has spent the first part of his childhood away from this home. Kailash is a much-storied peak in the Himalayas, alternately known as Mount Meru and Gang Rinpoche ('precious jewel of snows' in Tibetan). Its many names are perhaps a testament to its importance across many religions (including Bon, Buddhism, Hinduism, Jainism) and the cultures stemming from them.

Here in Canada, the festival takes on a different form – a gathering of Greater Toronto's comparatively small Maharashtrian community at the home of family friends who have installed an idol of Ganapati for the duration of the festivities. The idol symbolizes his annual descent from Kailash and onto the plains of humanity. There is a nightly potluck of food, prayer, camaraderie, and sartorial finery. Modaks definitely make an appearance, though unsurprisingly, not every night (#twentyfirstcenturylife).

Sandwiched between the end of summer and the rush of fall, with its ever-darkening days, Ganesh Chaturthi typically spans almost two entire weeks of the busiest time of work. I've come to see this event as a reminder of myself at a level far more fundamental than citizenships and nationalities. During the pandemic, through digital celebrations over video calls and Spotify playlists, Ganesh Chaturthi also became a way to understand that obstacles emerge and perhaps they fade, but we carry on.

With the filling bubbling on the stove, I turn now to the dough for the outer shell, emboldened by the fragrance of cardamom-laced coconut in the air. But I promptly realize I don't have the mould – that Hershey's Kisses–shaped thing that gives a modak its quintessential shape. To be fair, a good modak mould is hard to find. My mother and I have both spent hours online in years past searching for a basic plastic replica of the aluminum originals, but none pass muster. So hand-formed modaks it will be.

A few YouTube tutorials and a couple of maternal phone calls later, I've divvied up the rice flour mixture (salt, ghee, and water) into twenty-one parts, naturally, and begin to flatten, pull, and shape. Soon it becomes apparent that this dough stage is a total disaster. In the time I've taken to learn the technique, the dough has dried and cracked. Dipping my fingers in water to moisten it only makes the mixture stickier. The final dumpling is more akin to a Koosh ball than any lotus-shaped structure.

Swearing, sweating, and struggling, I just want to get to the finish line. I can't tell if the tears falling from my eyes are a cause or consequence of the irony of the situation: that an offering to the 'remover of obstacles' is, in fact, rife with them. As I shut the lid of the pressure cooker, the twenty-one modaks now steaming within, I'm still unsure about any of it: Why this now and why this way?

My mother calls to check in. As I fumble over the descriptions of my kitchen catastrophe, she listens quietly until finally she breaks the silence with a chuckle. I imagine an accompanying head shake, one that I know well.

'What?' I say.

'Your grandma would be proud,' she responds. 'The first time she had me make them, I threw out the dough six times. We ended up getting the takeout version.'

'You never told me that. Yours always come out right.'

'Yes, well, it's like that duck paddling on a lake. What you don't see … '

When I hang up, it's *my* head that shakes. The pressure cooker whistles – the sound of a triumphant elephant trumpeting victory. As I break apart the first steaming modak – lopsided, off-kilter, drizzled with ghee – I close my eyes in the bliss of the first bite.

It's a feeling, it's a feeling.

Wonton of Joy

Arlene Chan

Of all the rooms in our family home, the one I loved the most was the kitchen. Dialling back in time, my memory reel always stops on treasured moments there. The hours of good food, laughter, and stories remain vivid. Until I was nine years old, we lived in the west end Toronto neighbourhood known as the Junction, above our fruit store. Eng's Produce provided us with a bountiful supply of fresh goods. While I had a cozy upbringing there, my parents eventually sold the business and, in 1959, opened the Kwong Chow Chop Suey Restaurant in Toronto's first Chinatown. We now had a bountiful supply of delicious Cantonese food.

We moved downtown so we could be close to the restaurant. Our house had more than enough space for my parents, my five siblings, and me. My mother, Jean Lumb, had the foresight to tear down walls to enlarge the kitchen, which became the heart and soul of our family life. Although we had both a dining room and a living room, it was the kitchen where we ate, entertained, greeted visitors, chatted with friends and relatives, played cards, and did our homework.

At the kitchen's centre was an oversize oblong table. My father sat at the head while my mom, older brothers, younger sisters – with their legs dangling under the table – and I took our usual seats. I have fond memories of eating Chinese, Canadian, Italian, and other cuisines. But there is one dish I return to again and again to this day. When I think about my ultimate comfort food, the food that takes me back to my childhood, the number one go-to is Chinese dumplings. Satisfying my craving is as easy as 1-2-3 when I wander the streets of Chinatown – even better, when I could still get them from my parents' restaurant. But the taste of homemade dumplings surpassed these choices hands down.

For the annual ritual of making dumplings for Chinese New Year, we gathered around that kitchen table. All I knew at the time was that we loved making and eating dumplings. What I didn't know was that dumplings had been created some two thousand years earlier, during the Han dynasty. As the story goes, Zhang Zhongjing, an eminent physician who was said to be the inventor of wontons, wanted to bring relief against frostbitten ears during the harsh winters. He folded fillings in dough and boiled them into what became known as dumplings. The symbolism of dumplings evolved from there. Because they look like oval, boat-shaped gold ingots – ancient Chinese money – they were considered to bring good luck and fortune for the New Year. They also represented the strength of family unity and togetherness.

The ingenuity of transforming meagre ingredients into a delicious and hearty meal with the help of a little flour and water has been adopted in nearly every culture. Dumplings come in all shapes and sizes, with different fillings, wrappers, and cooking methods. Pierogies, momos, samosas, empanadas, and ravioli all come to mind. In Chinese culture, there is no shortage of varieties, depending on their place of origin within China. Dim sum alone encompasses over twenty kinds of dumplings. Wheat or rice flour dough. Sweet or savoury.

Leavened or unleavened. Pan-fried, deep-fried, steamed, boiled, or baked.

Wontons were the dumpling of choice for our family tradition. These are a Cantonese staple of southern Chinese culture and places like my parents' ancestral Guangdong province. Making wontons is not a complicated process. Although dumplings are filled with a countless variety of ingredients, ours were always the same: minced pork, green onions, ginger, cornstarch, salt, sugar, white pepper, sesame oil, soya sauce, and Chinese cooking wine. Add a bit of this, then some of that. No need to use measuring cups and such. Just eyeball it. Mix. Spoon onto the wrapper. Fill, fold, and boil.

We used ready-made wonton wrappers, also called wonton skins. Even though wrappers can be easily made with flour, water, and salt, beginner hands are challenged in rolling and cutting the dough into thin, even squares. There's no shame in using store-bought wrappers that are purchased frozen or refrigerated. We had our share of boxed mac and cheese, purchased by the case to feed six hungry kids — a working mom is a working mom.

Jean's time in the kitchen was limited by commitments, not only to her restaurant, but also to her community activism. She directed the dumpling-making sessions with the same determination and self-confidence as she pursued her goal to change Canada's immigration laws, which discriminated against Chinese newcomers and their families, or to lead the campaign to Save Chinatown.

My mother heaped praise on our finesse in making wontons. We held each square wrapper flat in the palm of one hand while the other scooped out a small amount of the pork mixture. After placing the filling carefully in the centre, we dipped a fingertip into water and ran it along the wrapper's edge. The next step involved closing the wonton into a triangular shape, then squeezing out the air and pressing on the edges. A tight seal was essential to keep the filling from seeping out or, even worse, exploding in the soup. My mother smiled with contentment as she presided over this time-honoured tradition. Who would dare eclipse dumpling-making skills that had been passed down for generations?

Only one person could. Ah Goo was regarded as our auntie because she came from Sunwui in Guangdong province, my father's birthplace. In Cantonese tradition, someone from the same ancestral county as a parent, for example, is considered a blood relative. *Goo* means aunt while *Ah* is added as a term of affection commonly used in southern China. Family members must be addressed using the correct terms. In English, *aunt* is the term of address for the sisters of both parents. In Chinese, however, there are no fewer than seven different words meaning aunt, depending on her marital status, the connection on your father's or mother's side, and whether she is younger or older than your parent.

Ah Goo would have been in her fifties when she set down roots down the street from our home. She was quite the auntie, with a sunny disposition and sense of humour that outshone the pranksterism of one of my brothers. She was always trying to fatten us up, reminding us never to waste any food, right down to the last grain of rice. If anyone wanted to get into her good books, asking for a second bowl of rice was the ticket.

Ah Goo was really the person in charge of our dumpling sessions, despite my mother's commanding presence. She was a harsh critic. Think of the film *Crazy Rich Asians*, when Rachel, the Chinese-American economics professor, is making dumplings under the disapproving gaze of her future mother-in-law. Ah Goo could be heard chiding us in her village dialect: Too big or too small! Too much filling or not enough! Not enough water to seal the edges! But we laughed when she found fault with how we folded the dumplings. 'Aiya!' Ah Goo exclaimed in a tone of exasperation that expressed her dismay with our lack of know-how. Our wontons were a far cry from hers, and from the ones at the Kwong Chow.

One lesson I learned from years of piano and tap-dancing lessons is that practice makes perfect. Wrapping dumplings can take years to master; many regard it as an art form. Take, as an example, Din Tai Fung, a world-renowned restaurant chain based in Taiwan. Its famed xiaolongbao dumplings, translated as 'small basket buns,' are wrapped with surgical precision. Each one has eighteen pleats that are gathered into a flourishing swirl at the top to encase the pork filling and hot soup. Thankfully, our version of wontons did not involve any pleats. In any event, what did Ah Goo expect from us when we wrapped dumplings only once a year?

Any shortcomings vanished when it came time to eat. After the wontons were parboiled in water, they were finished in a homemade broth. What can be more comforting on a cold winter day than dumplings in a steaming bowl of soup, sprinkled with chopped green onions? The sight of each one floating in the broth, like a fluffy cloud in the sky, explains why *wonton* translates as 'swallowing a cloud.' The translucent and silky-smooth skin barely contained the filling. Every bite packed an explosion of flavour and deliciousness. Sitting around the table, making dumplings, and sharing them connected us to the importance of family and togetherness. My mother always said, 'No matter what, family comes first.' Ah Goo didn't have to tell us. Under that feisty and outspoken persona was an auntie who loved her family without saying so.

Over the phases of my life and career – as a mother, grandmother, librarian, and writer – distant memories have surfaced in my consciousness. Many of these moments seem unremarkable but turn out to have deeper significance with the passing of each birthday. I find myself drawn back to that kitchen table, and my number one comfort food. I enjoy eating dumplings year-round. Connecting me to my family, my past, my roots, they never fail to give me one ton of joy.

Potatoes, Beans, and a Reluctant Cook

Chantal Braganza

While raising two children in Mississauga in the 1990s, my father was spoiled with choices when it came to feeding us the food he loved. At the time, this Toronto suburb was a fraction of the diverse behemoth it has since grown into. Nonetheless, Mississauga was still home to a thriving ecosystem of businesses serving up regional Indian cuisines: steaming foil bags of Crayola-red tandoori chicken; foam plastic dinner trays of thalis with every variation of dal we could name; boxes of fudgy, milk-based sweets soaked in syrup and laced with crushed nuts and edible silver foil; and so on. Seemingly every style of Indian takeout was available to him at that time and place, except the Goan food my father had grown up eating.

Much like the west coast state from where it originates, Goan cuisine occupies an interesting place in what we now call India. It is distinct in its flavours and ingredients, leaning heavily toward seafood and vinegar, and Goa is one of the first regions outside of the Americas to employ in its cuisine tomatoes, potatoes, and chili peppers – foods introduced via trade routes from 456 years of Portuguese occupation.

These are the kinds of details my father likes to remind me of – his way of passing food knowledge down, since his own childhood in coastal Kenya's Goan expat community had few memories of home-cooked meals. His home life was chaotic, and he found himself on his own at sixteen, until his family reunited in Toronto in the late 1970s.

However, one thing his mother, whom I called Nana, passed down to my dad was a one-dish obsession when it comes to cooking. For Nana, that dish was known as 'potato chops' – dumpling-like patties of mashed potato stuffed with spiced ground beef, dredged in egg and bread crumbs, then pan-fried until crisp. She rarely cooked anything else, in fact, so my dad ate potato chops for dinner and rice pudding for dessert through most of his childhood. Understandably, he got sick of both and he never once looked back fondly on either of those foods when he became a parent himself.

Maybe his disdain for potato chops explains why I remember so clearly the only time Nana cooked them for my brother and me. We were eight and nine respectively, and she lived in a one-bedroom, retirement-living apartment in Mississauga at the time. More often than not, her kitchen was stocked with the best of snacks: frozen chicken pot pies, jars of cashews, bags of Bugles, and cans of ketchup-flavoured Pringles. One weekend afternoon, our parents dropped us off at her home, and she cooked my brother and me potato chops in her little kitchen. The mashed potatoes and ground beef filling had already been prepared when we arrived. All that was left to do was form the mash into dough-like pockets and stuff them with meat before dredging, frying, and serving them with a squirt of Heinz on disposable blue plastic plates.

The meal came as a surprise to us – a home-cooked luxury, rendered as such because potato chops were a rare occurrence in our house and almost never spoken of. Nana may not have cooked much, but she had the method for preparing this particular dish down to a science: spicy vinegared beef wrapped in a salty crunch, not unlike a chicken nugget. That was the only time I tried her version of the dish and one of very few instances I have had potato chops since then.

Until I started trying to make them myself.

Doing so helped me to understand a lot about my grandmother's and father's respective personalities. Functionally, potato chops require a lot of active attention: boiling and mashing potatoes, cooking the spiced filling, assembling the chops, dredging them in egg and bread crumbs, then shallow-frying them until crisp. There is no extended resting time or long simmer on a stove. They are most often cooked as comfort meals or a party treat and make for an odd choice as a frequent weeknight dinner.

It didn't dawn on me until after she passed that Nana didn't cook them as often as she did because they were easy for the reluctant cook. Rather, she loved them enough to take the time to make them often – sometimes even at the expense of her children's enjoyment of dinner. A younger version of me might have regarded this habit uncharitably or seen it as selfish, but I think her perseverance was its own gesture of love.

Like his mother, my father was always confounded by cooking – hence the takeout – except when it came to dried beans. Black beans, pinto beans, cranberry, lima. If these legumes could be cooked with an onion and a garlic clove in a pot of water, you can bet my father made a soup out of them. It took him years to learn the tricks of dried beans – about the soak and boil times and the seasoning they required.

Consequently, his bean soups were often thin and under-cooked, with rafts of waterlogged onion floating in the broth.

'My faaaamous bean soup!' he'd chirp any night my mom wasn't able to make dinner, which wasn't often, but frequent enough for my brother and me to decide early on that we hated bean soup and possibly just beans in general.

My father grew up as the sibling who was at odds with his mother. I grew up having the same relationship with my father in my early life (and, to be honest, sometimes still). And so, for a long time, I never once looked back fondly on his bean concoctions. Even when I learned to feed myself, even after I grew into a person who loves to cook, unlike him and his mother before him. For years, the idea of using dried beans over canned seemed more like a barrier to a home-cooked meal than a delicious end goal in and of itself. In some cases, I think this assumption still holds true. But I've mostly come around when it comes to using dried beans over canned, and the period of pandemic-enforced home cooking, in particular, proved how wrong I had been.

I've also been lucky enough to learn tricks of my own when it comes to dried beans: cooking them on a hard boil for ten minutes before simmering or using baking soda to speed up the process, and always salting them at the *end* of cooking. Perfect, articulated, smooth-as-cream legumes every time. I'll spice them with flavours that transform the beans into an approximation of any dish I want: bacon and red wine for bourguignon; tomato paste, olives, capers, and anchovies for a puttanesca; avocado leaf and cumin for a salsa, madre-based soup. Learning how to cook beans prop-erly, in fact, made me a better cook overall. And yet there is almost no version of them I can cook that will consistently entice my own two young children to eat, let alone enjoy, them. The lesson is not lost on me, though my father has been graceful enough never to point it out; he brings them their favourite takeout instead.

The version of potato chop I'm sharing below swaps out the vinegared beef with black beans, cooked the way I prepare them for soup. This version is far from traditional, but it's also a good example of how the way we cook evolves; it reconciles dish, ingredients, and a little light obsession into something that feels right for me.

BLACK BEAN POTATO CHOPS

BLACK BEANS
1 cup dried black beans, rinsed
¼ tsp baking soda
1 bay leaf
½ onion, intact
2 cloves garlic, peeled and smashed
1 bird's eye chili, split halfway but still attached at the stem
1 tsp cumin seeds
½ tsp salt

1. Cover rinsed beans with 3 cups cold water in a pot. Set aside to soak overnight.
2. Transfer pot to stovetop, stir in baking soda, and, without changing the water, bring pot to a hard boil for 10 minutes, then reduce heat to a simmer.
3. Add bay leaf, onion, garlic, cumin seeds, and bird's eye chili; cover pot and continue to simmer until beans are tender, about 60 minutes. If beans are still undercooked, continue to check them (adding water as necessary) every

10 minutes until done. Remove bay leaf, onion half, chili, and garlic cloves, if they are still intact. (If they've completely fallen apart, they can be mixed into the beans and cooking liquid; they'll incorporate quickly.)

4. Using a fork or potato masher, crush the beans into the cooking water until mostly mashed and water is incorporated. Alternately, blend beans and cooking liquid together until it becomes a thick purée.

Bean mixture can be made ahead and will keep covered in the fridge for up to three days. It will continue to thicken.

POTATO CHOPS

3 medium russet potatoes, peeled and roughly chopped
1 tsp salt
1 Tbsp olive oil
2 cups black bean mixture, room temperature
2 large eggs, beaten
1½ cups Panko bread crumbs
5 Tbsp vegetable frying oil, such as canola

1. Cover potatoes with cold water in a stock pot and bring to a boil. Cook for 10 to 15 minutes until fork-tender, then drain. Pass potatoes through a ricer, mix with salt and olive oil, and set aside. This can be made up to one day ahead and kept in the fridge.

2. Scoop mashed potatoes into palm-sized mounds, shape each one into a ½-inch thick disc, and press a hollow indentation in the centre with your thumb.

3. Drop a heaping tablespoon of bean mixture in the indentation and gently press the outer edges of the potato disc

up and over the bean mash, forming it into a patty-shaped disc. Continue until no more mashed potato remains.

4. Dredge each patty in the beaten-egg wash, then the bread crumbs. Shallow-fry in vegetable oil on each side for 1 to 2 minutes until golden brown. Drain on a plate lined with paper towel and serve warm.

Note: Use any leftover bean mixture as a taco filling or toast spread, or thin out with piping-hot vegetable stock until desired consistency for one to two servings of black bean soup.

The Hong Kong Bakery's Magic Door

Naomi Duguid

In the mid-1970s, I moved to Toronto to go to law school, and a few months later I started to learn tai chi. Madame Tsang, the instructor, taught three afternoons a week in the large hall of St. Paul's–Avenue Road, a beautiful heritage church that arsonists burned down in the 1990s. Then in her seventies, Madame Tsang, a small, erect figure in loose black trousers, who always looked perfectly grounded and in balance, would lead us through the form. She relied on showing us rather than talking. We all wore cotton tai chi slippers that allowed us to step deliberately and almost silently through the form. The calm and quiet were a welcome contrast to the torrents of words that flowed at the law school just down the road.

Sometime in my second year, Madame Tsang invited me to come with her to Dundas Street for dim sum. It was my introduction to the Hong Kong Bakery, a tiny storefront behind City Hall with a front window set at an angle to the sidewalk. It was family-run, unfancy, and intimate, with just a few tables. The food came fresh and hot from the kitchen: perfect, delicate har gao; large soup dumplings, one per bowl, with their fine skin and elegant seam, and a little dish of ginger shreds in vinegar as accompaniment; tofu skin rolls, succulent and slightly chewy-crispy; stuffed rice noodles, tender and slippery and dressed with a splash of lightly vinegared soy sauce.

My memory of that first visit with Madame Tsang is now overlaid with the many more times I went back to the Hong Kong through the late 1970s and early 1980s, often with a friend or two. As a group, we could taste more dishes. The narrow shopfront was so insignificant-looking that I'd often walk right past it before realizing I'd missed it. Unlike larger dim sum places, there were no carts at the Hong Kong, and nothing had been cooked ahead of time. Instead, you were handed a pencil stub and small sheet of paper with a list of dishes printed in red in both Chinese characters and English transcriptions of the Cantonese names: har gao, siu mai, sin chut kuen, cheung fun, fun gok, and more. We marked off the ones we wanted to try. Most menu items cost only a dollar. It took serious eating for two people to push the bill over ten dollars.

I liked the siu mai and the nor mi gai (sticky rice with Chinese sausage and chicken, all steamed in an aromatic lotus leaf) – a treat so filling you need other people to share it with. But the outstanding items were the large, supple soup dumplings and the delicate har gao, three to a steamer. To eat your soup dumpling, which sat steaming plumply in its bowl, you had to tear a small hole in the top, pour in a little dipping sauce, then spoon up the soup and some of the fine wrapper dough, mouthful by mouthful. The dumplings seemed miraculous; only many years later did I learn how they were made.

As for the har gao: I've rarely had a har gao that compares. They were delicately perfect, nearly transparent rice noodle wrappers enclosing tender pink shrimp. As you bit down, there was the yielding texture of the shrimp and a mild crunch from a little slice of water chestnut. The har gao needed to be eaten as soon as they were placed on the table, hot hot, before they oversteamed or cooled down. The steamers were traditional bamboo rounds, with that evocative aroma of moist, steamy bamboo when you lifted off the lid.

A few years after I first went to the Hong Kong, my friend Cassandra and I decided to try to make jiaozi, basic potsticker dumplings, which are first cousins of Japanese gyoza. We wanted to see if we could produce non-meat ones – filled with spiced and flavoured gluten – that would be as delectable as the classic pork-filled jiaozi. We went out and bought ground pork and some strong (high gluten) bread flour, as well as all-purpose flour.

We made a simple dough with the all-purpose flour, which we kneaded until very smooth and then set aside to rest. We massaged and rinsed handfuls of the strong flour with water to wash away the starch and amazingly ended up with a mass of gluten. (We had to make our own because in those days gluten wasn't easy to find in stores.) We flavoured both the gluten and the ground pork with salt, soy sauce, minced ginger, garlic, and minced green onions, seasoning the gluten mixture a little more heavily. Then we cut the rested dough into several pieces, rolled each out into a thin sheet, and cut out circles, our wrappers.

Shaping dumplings takes skill. For jiaozi, you lay a wrapper on a lightly floured surface and run a wet finger around the edge to moisten it slightly. Then on goes a little filling. The hard part comes next: you fold the dough over the filling, pinch it together at the centre of the curve, then use your thumb and finger to pleat the dough all along the edge to seal it. Not so simple! My fingers felt very clumsy, and my first dumplings were a mess. But slowly the process became familiar, and the dumplings started to shape themselves. We ended up with dumplings that weren't elegant, but were at least recognizably jiaozi-shaped.

Once we had our dumplings formed, some filled with the gluten mixture and some with the pork, it was time to cook them. Potstickers get put into a hot, lightly oiled skillet, where they start browning. You add a little hot water to the skillet, the lid goes on, and they steam for a minute or two before the lid comes back off. Then they cook a minute or more longer as the water boils away, leaving them browned, cooked through, and succulent.

Our experiment was a big success: we had trouble telling the difference between the taste and texture of the pork and the vegetarian ones. But more amazing was the understanding I gained of how much work and skill goes into each little dumpling.

Alas, at some point in the mid-1980s, the Hong Kong closed. The owners opened a restaurant-style place around the corner, just off Dundas, but the perfectly fresh dumplings were no more. Soon afterwards that restaurant closed, too.

There was another small, family-run dumpling spot near downtown, even more homemade in feel, which only partly filled the gap left when the Hong Kong closed. At the Ko family bakery, on Baldwin Street about ten minutes west, you could order the basics: har gao and siu mai, as well as a few other dumplings, along with baozi and custard tarts, to eat at a small table inside or outside. The bakery was an inexpensive, reliable go-to place for students and others in the area until it too closed, some years ago.

Times change. There are losses, but also gains. In the last twenty-plus years, other dumpling places, such as Yummy Yummy Dumplings and Mother's Dumplings, have sprung up in downtown Toronto and elsewhere. They're a great addition to the dumpling scene and fill an important niche. They make hearty northern-style dumplings – wheat-flour wrappers filled with ground pork (or other meat) flavoured with aromatics –

rather like the jiaozi Cassandra and I experimented with long ago. The dumplings are served boiled, steamed, or fried, or sold by the dozen, frozen, to be cooked at home. An intensely flavoured dipping sauce of black vinegar with soy sauce, with an optional touch of chili oil, is the usual complement.

For a long time now, my favourite local source for southern Chinese-style dumplings has been the array of dim sum offerings at Sky Dragon, on the top floor of Dragon City, at Dundas and Spadina. It's a large space, but still welcoming and lively. Until recently the carts at Sky Dragon were wheeled around by servers who had been there for years. They'd patiently lift the lids off the steamers on their carts to show you the dumplings and other treats on offer, in case you hadn't understood the names they'd called out as they approached. These days instead you choose from an illustrated menu and the dishes come hot and fresh to the table.

I feel so lucky to have entered the world of dumplings via the magic door of the Hong Kong Bakery. That world is going strong in Toronto and still evolving. Dumplings shaped by hand, carefully steamed or fried, picked up one at a time with chopsticks, lifted to the mouth, then eaten with pleasure, are being made and enjoyed all over the city and across the Greater Toronto Area. When I think back to that first visit to the Hong Kong, and then reflect on the hundreds of dumplings I've eaten since, I picture the deft hands, the various fillings, the fine rice- or wheat- or tapioca-flour wrappers, the choices of dipping sauces, and I marvel at the landscape of delicious possibilities unfolding in my mind's eye. Respect!

The Knedlík, Warts and All

Eric Geringas

W hen the Berlin Wall fell in late 1989, I was in my final year of university, churning out papers on obscure topics in political philosophy. And, of course, like most everyone else, I became glued to news of the crumbling Iron Curtain. My friends and I watched in wonder as ordinary people stood up and demanded their freedom, and one Communist regime after another just ... gave up and resigned.

It happened quietly in Hungary, brutally in Romania, and most wonderfully and romantically in Czechoslovakia, where tens of thousands of people filled historic Wenceslas Square, and the absurdist playwright Václav Havel appeared on a balcony to address the masses. 'We want to live as a free and dignified people,' he said – a simple demand that more than once had landed him in prison. But now the time had come.

Within months, Havel was president, and the country was ruled not by grey apparatchiks, but by intellectuals, ex-journalists, and fans of the Velvet Underground.

Here in Canada, as I contemplated my next move after finally completing my BA, an irresistible opportunity presented itself: a group of Czech émigrés had put together an organization, immodestly called Education for Democracy, that would bring Canadians to Czechoslovakia to teach English. Hundreds of young people rushed to sign up, eager for adventure and a front-row seat to history.

And that's how I ended up, in the fall of 1990, boarding a plane and heading to what just months before had been a closed society, a place untouched by Western conveniences or consumer goods, or really anything invented after 1968.

I'd heard about the excellent Czech beer, but I had no idea what I'd be eating.

Fast-forward two weeks, and I am living in Prague, a city where even the pollution is gorgeous – the coal dust in the air gives the street lamps the kind of magical aura that wins Oscars for cinematographers. Central Prague is stuck in time, completely untouched by modern development, and apparently not cleaned since Franz Kafka haunted its alleyways. You can feel you're walking in the early twentieth century, then turn a corner and find yourself in the seventeenth. The prices, too, are from the early twentieth century – that excellent Czech beer costs just fifteen cents a half-litre. I quickly discover its magical properties: part lubricant, part glue, it fuels many long evenings with new friends.

I start my job, at – of all places – the General University Hospital, a rambling campus of crumbling buildings in central Prague. I've been assigned a group of eager students – doctors, administrators, orderlies. For my efforts, I am to get a couple hundred dollars a month, plus room and board with a lovely young family, and – an unexpected perk – lunch at the hospital.

The country I'm falling in love with is about to show me what it means to love something warts and all.

On my first day on the job, I show up at the staff cafeteria for lunch and am given a large plate of some kind of brown stew, served with some white things the shape and diameter of slices of baguette. The stew is heavy, but bearable. Just. I grew up with East European food – I'm not expecting vindaloo. But the white slices, which I can see are supposed to absorb the sauce from the stew … it's like chewing wet cardboard.

My students laugh when I tell them about my lunch. 'Ah, knedlíky! Czech dumplings! Very traditional! Very tasty!'

Dumplings? I love dumplings! My parents used to get frozen pelmeni and vareniki from a Russian lady uptown. I'm from Toronto – I know har gao from siu mai. How are those delicious morsels related to *this*? These lumps of starch are not stuffed with little bits of delicious filling. They are just … stale bread mixed with wallpaper paste and boiled.

You think I'm kidding? Okay, maybe not wallpaper paste. But definitely stale bread – boiled in a mixture of milk, eggs, flour, and salt, then sliced.

Talk about poverty cuisine. Later, I try to find out how this abomination came to be. Unsurprisingly, no one really knows. One story is that they were first made by an eighteenth-century army cook after his oven was destroyed by enemy fire. But mostly, people think the Czech bread dumpling dates back to the Middle Ages – peasants trying to make the most of what they had.

For the next three months, four times a week, I take a long streetcar and metro ride to the hospital, and try to give these friendly, eager Czechs some confidence in speaking the English they learned in high school. Before every class, I go to the desultory hospital cafeteria and hope that this day's starch is potatoes – boiled, mashed, or fried, they are always better than boiled stale bread. The cafeteria ladies know me as the Canadian who always reminds them, *'Ne knedlíky'* – no dumplings, please.

In class, I play pop songs on the little portable cassette player I brought from home, and we study the lyrics. I teach them weird English idioms, such as euphemisms for throwing up – phrases they will have absolutely no use for, even working in a hospital. (Did I really think this vocabulary was going to be helpful to the doctors? 'I understand, Mr. Tourist. You spent the night praying to the porcelain god. Let's get you some fluids.')

I spend the rest of my time hanging out with a motley collection of friends – some Czech, some Canadian and American. Most of us North Americans are new university grads looking for our place in the world, taking our gap year *after* getting our BAs. The Czechs in our group – of various ages – are kind of in the same place. With the end of Communist rule, the world has suddenly opened up for them, their future unexpectedly unwritten. They can travel, pursue new careers, start something of their own – do whatever they want. And they, too, are taking a gap year to figure it out.

My teaching contract comes to an end around Christmas, but I stay on in Prague for a few months longer. Czechoslovakia is both strangely familiar – I spent the first seven years of my life not far from there, in Soviet-occupied Latvia – and profoundly different.

It's the early 1990s. There's no internet. Phone calls home are unaffordable. News in English is available mainly via the *Guardian* and the *International Herald Tribune*, sold in a few places in town for the price of six beers. The comforts of home – things like breakfast cereal and ketchup, the music we listen to, shoes that are not made in State Factory #7 – all of this is starting to trickle in, but only bit by bit. As new things appear on store shelves, we North Americans get just as excited as the locals, and learn to share information about where to find a salad bar, or which shop has German muesli.

Gradually, I learn more about this place I'm a guest in. I can't quite put my finger on why Prague is so much more attractive to me than the various other European capitals – Paris, London, and especially nearby Vienna, the former seat of the Austro-Hungarian Empire, with its gaudy palaces and well-scrubbed cobblestones.

And then it comes to me. Prague was never an imperial capital. From the sixteenth century until the end of the First World War, it was a provincial city – part of the Habsburg Empire, but never a regional pinnacle of power or the recipient of massive imperial wealth. What I fell in love with about Czech culture – the black humour, the winking anti-authoritarianism – grew under centuries of Austrian rule and then withstood forty years of Soviet totalitarianism. This is a culture of survival, of learning to thrive even when power is in someone else's hands. The humble bread dumpling – the most basic survival food – is just as central to the Czechs' identity as their most famous literary character, the bumbling Good Soldier Švejk, who embodies passive resistance to distant imperial authority, serving incompetently in the Austro-Hungarian army.

In the end, no one manages to convince me that Czech dumplings are anything more than stale bread boiled in wallpaper paste, though many people try. Having grown up in Toronto – where peasant food is Chinese and Korean, Italian and Caribbean – I know that 'poor' absolutely does not have to equal bland. But I do develop some grudging respect for the lowly knedlík. It is to fancy imperial cuisine what the Good Soldier Švejk is to imperial power – a middle finger to pomposity and entitlement. And to that I can raise a glass of excellent Czech beer.

I Pinch, Therefore I Am

Matthew Murtagh-Wu

Dumplings have come to play a major role in defining me as a person. That sounds a bit weird as I read that sentence back to myself. But it's true: I am and own the Dumpling King, a micro food production company in East Vancouver. Between 2015 and 2022, my little dumpling-pinching operation has folded and sold over 650,000 handmade frozen dumplings. I also source as many ingredients as I can from the old vendors of Vancouver's Chinatown.

I run my company out of a shared commercial kitchen. It's home to a wide range of other small food businesses purveying products and services, from private fine dining to koji, fresh pasta, bento boxes, and Nigerian suya. Amid this maelstrom of entrepreneurial chaos, my dead-simple, hand-made dumpling production line operates out of a three-by-one-and-a-half-metre patch of concrete, with a work table, a freezer, and a couple of forks. Every morning between 9:00 and 9:30 a.m., one of my butchers in Chinatown delivers dozens of kilos of freshly ground pork belly to the back-alley bay doors of my kitchen. My team and I process and season the meat, hand-mixing to a proprietary guideline. We then pinch and fold thousands of dumplings.

By mid-afternoon, the freezer is locked and the station is cleaned, with the dumplings left overnight to freeze. The following morning, I bag and deliver them to local cafés, grocers, restaurants, and butcher shops across the Lower Mainland. Despite hawking only three flavours (all pork), the Dumpling King has metamorphosed from a 24/7, one-man dumpling delivery service and travelling pop-up restaurant into its current incarnation as a 'mass production' hand-made dumpling manufacturer, with a social media brand and persona.

This whole entrepreneurial thing is surreal, hilarious, rewarding, and terrifying – all at the same time. What started as a way of expressing my heritage and culinary skill as a Chinese Canadian has evolved into a full-fledged business that pays taxes. I've spent so much time selling, delivering, folding, and worrying over dumplings that it feels as if they have irreversibly rewired my brain.

It wasn't always like this, though. In 2015, I quit a low-level position at a bank, where I'd spent four repetitive years pushing credit cards, travel insurance, and foreign exchange. The monotony was interrupted only by encounters with the public's understandable disgust and annoyance with large financial institutions. The bank expected me to sell and, if I could, build enough of a rapport with a customer that they might be open to speaking with one of the mortgage brokers, financial planners, or estate specialists working one floor above me. If the referral closed in a sale, I'd sometimes receive a Tim Horton's gift card for being a good boy.

On my lunch breaks, I wondered why I wasn't particularly stoked about my job and the opportunity to build a sensible career at a bank. Yet to me, the work never felt right and I

didn't like the person I was becoming. Everyone, including myself, had been reduced to numbers and calculations used to assess net worth and calculate risk. I'd sit on the bus ride back home, trying to balance a moral and existential equation that would never ever make sense.

During this time, my ma ma (paternal grandmother) died suddenly, just a couple of months past her eightieth birthday. We discovered her in her apartment on a Saturday morning after she didn't respond to phone calls for three days. She had had a heart attack. Her groceries were still at the foot of the sofa by the front door, just as she had left them. The siu choy in her grocery bag was wilted. Less than two paces away, in the bedroom, I saw my grandmother's lifeless form, face down on her bedroom floor. Her slippers were still on and so were all the lights. She must have died in the evening.

At work one day not long after her death, and still mourning, I calculated how many years, months, weeks, days, and hours I had left in my tank if I were to make it to her age. I felt traumatized: the number I came up with was about eighteen thousand days. I gave notice to my manager.

Immediately after leaving the bank, I tried my luck again in the financial field by working for a venture capitalist. We rented a single room in an office space two blocks down from my previous employer. Our desks pushed together, we sat face to face, crammed into an office fit for one person. For four months, I spent my time learning about the British Columbian softwood industry and how much two-by-fours went for in the Asian market. I'd make and send off investor pitch decks, trying to convince rich people that our financially unviable goal of flipping Canadian softwood and selling it to Japanese and Chinese markets would result in a profit for all involved. We'd muse every other day about what we would do if we each won a million dollars. I told my boss I'd cook.

After I hadn't been paid for three months, the money ran out and I realized I didn't need a million dollars to do what I had always wanted. So I applied to and graduated from culinary school and immediately entered the kitchen. For two years, I bounced around cooking gigs all over Vancouver: scrubbing deep fryers and washing dishes, acting as prep drone, making curries at a Thai restaurant, forming falafel and plating tabbouleh at a Lebanese restaurant. At the same time, I was trying to grow my own book of clients as a private chef.

It was back-breaking work. On one shift, I managed to put a blade through every single digit on my left hand. My chef bought me a beer. Closing the night shift at another job, I dragged out the trash while balancing a stack of flattened cardboard boxes so I didn't have to make two trips (of course). Each night, I'd think the same thoughts to myself: 'Eighteen thousand or so more days left. You've squandered an opportunity for a stable career and seven years of post-secondary education, and all you got is just *one hand* that isn't covered in Band-Aids and finger condoms – and for what?'

As with that bank job, I again felt I was not making the most of my ever-dwindling, death-day count. During my off-hours, I began to fiddle in my home kitchen, trying to recreate the dishes from my increasingly fading memories of child-hood: bok choy fried rice with Jinhua ham, soy sauce–braised 'lion's head' meatballs, steamed fish, and kao fu (chilled wheat gluten with fungus and lily stems in an herbal gravy). These were all dishes that formed core memories of growing up. They were the no-frills, gently seasoned cooking of my grand-mother, and I sought inspiration from these recipes.

I remember how, when I was younger and my parents had gone out of town, my ma ma would cook just for me. She would drop off a tightly wrapped, used grocery bag of Tupperware containers full of her homestyle Shanghainese cooking. The bag always had a thoughtfully folded dishcloth or piece of newspaper between the containers. It would be hidden by the stairs near the back door. She'd never knock, preferring just to leave a brief voice mail on my cell, telling me in her broken English that she'd left something for me.

I continued to fiddle in my kitchen until I realized that making dumplings was a way for me to stop my mind from anxiously spinning. Making dumplings was meditative, but at the same time a potentially promising first-time entrepre-neurial endeavour. If they didn't sell, I'd just keep them in the freezer until they did. Everyone loves dumplings, right?

I put the word out on social media, pitching to my circle of friends that I was making some dumplings using ingredients from Vancouver's Chinatown and I would deliver to them. Instantly, the reception was huge. Over the months, word travelled, and a local publication covered me. I provided my cellphone number in the article, and once it was published, my phone started lighting up: 'Hey, man, you the guy who makes and delivers dumplings? Can I get a couple bags? I live near Science World.' It was then that I realized I was onto something. I delivered my handmade frozen dumplings alone for nearly four years, non-stop. There have since been thousands of customers and even more dumplings.

People still ask me if the recipe for my dumplings is my grandmother's or if it's some guarded family recipe that's been passed down through the generations. The answer is 'No, it's not.' The dumplings my customers purchase in 2022 are simply the result of a lost person attempting to create something from nostalgia with whatever ingredients he had in his pantry at the time. Everything else after that was just repetition. So yes, I can unequivocally state that dumplings have defined me in ways I never could have imagined. And it was the loss of my grandmother that ultimately inspired me to start making them.

Heavy Is the Head That Wears the Pierogi Crown

Monika Warzecha

I don't mean to brag, but I come from dumpling royalty. Immediately after my sister's Grade 8 graduation from our Catholic elementary school in Toronto, her teacher set up a small ceremony in the church basement. Each student was presented with a joke gift or award. Young and energetic, a figure of fun, the teacher often brought up the fact that my sister was Polish. And so, when my sister joined him onstage, he gave her a tinfoil wand and a pink bristol-board crown with two pierogi stapled alongside the words 'Pierogi Princess.' After all, what's more Polish than pierogi?

When my sister took her seat, my family inspected the crown. It had grease marks. The pierogi were fully cooked. We found it all a little funny and weird, maybe even a bit sacrilegious for the waste of perfectly good food.

Family bloodlines, then, would indicate that I, too, am a pierogi princess. For anyone who would contest my claim, I present this additional evidence: my last name, depending on who you ask, translates to either *ladle* or *wooden spoon*, an important utensil for pierogi cooking; I spent a large part of my formative years watching my grandmother make pierogi;

I spent a large part of my formative years mimicking the pierogi-production process with playdough; I once travelled to Poland and ate bona-fide old-country pierogi; I have hunted down every available pierogi source in my East Toronto neighbourhood; I'm pretty sure I would die if I stopped eating carbs.

Like many hyphenated Canadians, I grew up feeling ambivalent about my background, pierogi and all. My parents immigrated as adults and I was born in Toronto. I often stressed the latter part in the multicultural classrooms I grew up in when the question of who came from where invariably came up. I was from here. But my nose and my last name often gave me away as not well and *truly* Canadian. At the time, I thought being Canadian meant having a vaguely Anglo background, or maybe French. Something where immigration and settlement were distant or forgotten pieces of family lore.

Now in my thirties, I'm comfortable with my heritage and cringe when I think back on how keen I was to distance myself from all things Polish. But it took some time, and a lot of dumplings, to get here.

Many of my early memories involve my grandmother. She took care of my sister and me while my parents were at work. I remember trips to a local park with picnics of poppyseed or honey cake. There were hours and hours spent in the kitchen while she made pierogi from scratch. The standbys in our household were pierogi filled with potato and cottage cheese, blueberries, kapusta, and occasionally buckwheat. This was before I started full-day school, and I remember those days as pleasant flashes: the kitchen full of sunshine and flour, cotton cloths and steam. I was proud of any small task I was given as busywork. I greedily ate the bits of fried dough my grand-mother would make from any leftover scraps.

This was Polish food before the Fall.

Newcomer children or first-generation Canadians have so many anecdotes about being teased about food that it's practically its own genre of storytelling: Kids Made Fun of My Ethnic Lunch. I'm certainly one of them. At my Toronto elementary school, even though pretty much everyone was from somewhere else, there was an abrupt shift against anything too Polish.

It was the early nineties, and my school absorbed a large number of children who had just moved here from post-Soviet Poland. A new ESL teacher joined the regular staff. I didn't want to be grouped with the new kids who didn't dress or speak right and who my friends eyed with cold suspicion or outright derision.

And so I refused to eat a lot of Polish fare at home. Special holiday meals or any dinner that involved food that might inspire hypothetical sneers from classmates became a battle-ground with my parents or grandma. Cabbage rolls? Nope. Pickled herring? Absolutely not. Barszcz? Ugh, if you strain out the chunks of vegetables, maybe – *maybe* – I'll have half a bowl.

But even then I could sense that pierogi were still some-how acceptable, an ethnic-food loophole. I still ate them at home, in part because dumplings served with fried onions, bacon lardons, sour cream, or melted butter are pretty much impossible to resist. The style of dumpling was also palatable to people who didn't grow up with them in Polish, Ukrainian, or Russian households. There was no soft cabbage or oily fish or slippery beets involved. And despite all the suspicion toward the newcomers, I remember a non-Polish peer bring-ing 'pizza pierogi' to a class potluck. The dumplings looked a little sinister to me. I don't know what they were stuffed with, but there was something dark at the heart of them. I didn't put any on my plate. I was careful.

By the time I reached high school, the Polish kids had melted into the school system, largely unremarked upon. And yet I still felt on guard.

Looking back, I think the overall feeling at the time was a touch classist in flavour. A girl in one of my classes, after hearing I was Polish, asked if I could call up her cleaning lady and tell her to wash a specific outfit for that evening. I worked various retail jobs in well-heeled western Toronto neighbourhoods in my teens, many of which had older Polish or Ukrainian communities at their core. It wasn't uncommon, working in a clothing store in Bloor West Village, to hear a customer in a moment of annoyance mutter, 'Stupid Polack,' at someone who had bumped into them. Once, when I was working in a bookshop along the Kingsway, one of our regulars, a doctor with a nearby office, told an agitated elderly woman who had entered the shop to go back to Poland. I never said anything.

Though I haven't heard a Polish joke in years, it can feel a little strange to have a nationality with a history of being treated like a punchline, where your ethnicity connotes a kind of mild stupidity: the butt of the joke always involves a dumb peasant, or rube, or working-class meathead. Working my way through an English degree while holding vague literary ambitions, I never denied my background or felt the same desperate desire for separation as I did when I was nine. But I didn't exactly embrace it either.

Then, while I was finishing my last year of university, my grandmother died. She of the floury hands and fried dough and poppyseed cake picnics and stories about Poland. In my grief, I turned toward what was left of our connection, my background and hers, with a vengeance.

I pestered my parents for details about life before immigration. Mesmerized by folk art, I tried and failed to teach myself embroidery. I shoved the fact of my heritage into conversation, often unprompted. I bought a book called *The Essential Guide to Being Polish*.

It took a surprisingly long time for me to realize I could actually visit the place my grandmother and parents came from without a time machine. No one in my family had gone back. It was like a door had closed on that world. Poland meant sad stories about war, black-and-white photos, forests and mushrooms, Communists, and Catholic rituals. The past was very much a foreign country. But in my late twenties, itching to travel during the off-peak autumn season, I bought a plane ticket and surprised my family.

I spent a few days with cousins in a small village in the western part of the country. Given their custom of starting with a larger meal and then tapering off with lighter foods throughout the day, I delightedly accepted a breakfast of pierogi with bacon one morning. I visited Gdansk, then spent a week in Krakow, meeting up with a friend who lived in London. It was an orgy of carbs: bagels, street-corner zapiekanki, open-face sandwiches with oscypek and cranberry preserves, and pierogi, dear God, the pierogi. We haunted a van Gogh–themed pierogi restaurant. When my friend returned to London the day before my return flight, I wandered around by myself, completely in love with the city. For my last meal in Poland, there was no question about what I would eat. I returned to Pierogi Mr Vincent and blissed out over a meal of dumplings stuffed with mushrooms and kapusta.

It can feel a bit confusing to see the full-scale Canadian embrace of all things pierogi, given how much of my younger years felt like a suppression of one side of my background in favour of the other. I have read op-eds that argued pierogi are a truly Canadian food, and reports about Canadian expats coming together to ferret out pierogi suppliers while living abroad in less pierogi-loving countries. The comfort-food aspect, the fast-and-cheap-and-filling adoption of the pierogi, doesn't bother me. Hell, there's even a 7.6-metre-tall pierogi statue in Alberta (I have not seen it, but I support it unreservedly). But I have to admit that when I first saw pierogi on the menus of a handful of buzzy restaurants in downtown Toronto, I sent a panicked text to a friend: 'Is Polish food cool now?!' I was also a little suspicious when a restaurant chain that offers pierogi topped with butter chicken or brisket or truffle oil started to expand with promises to hip up their locations.

I should probably just chalk it up as a good sign. Perhaps someone is writing a thesis right now on how the rise of pierogi – in restaurants and the frozen food section of grocery stores – reflects the overall success of the Polish diaspora in Canada.

I will gladly eat store-brand cheddar pierogi pulled from the depths of the grocery store freezer on nights when I don't feel like cooking. I have been to bars where pierogi are served nacho-style with salsa and melted cheese. I will try whatever novelty filling comes my way, whether it involves jalapenos or, yes, pizza-like ingredients. But the plate of food that will live on as my favourite meal is the one I had alone in a restaurant in Krakow. I'm no purist, but there's a reason the classics are classics.

No one has yet offered to anoint me a pierogi princess. However, I am secure enough now to say that I will gladly seize the crown, Napoleon-style, melted butter streaming down my face as I bestow the most Polish of Polish titles upon myself.

The Case for Kreplach

Bev Katz Rosenbaum

By now, dear readers, you will have read a fair bit about the ubiquitous knaidl, or matzo ball. Now it's time for you to learn about that dumpling's criminally overlooked sibling, the krepele (plural: kreplach). I have long been a lover of this unsung dumpling, commonly made by wrapping a chopped- or minced-meat mixture in a soft, pasta/wonton-like dough, then poaching it in soup (though it can also be fried). It's a far superior doughy treat, in my humble opinion, to the matzo ball, which ranks right down there with sponge cake (a cake that tastes like a sponge – lord, save us) as a Jewish delicacy. And yet, all we hear is matzo ball, matzo ball, matzo ball!

Feh. Younger cooks – like my son, who's worked at several high-end restaurants and ran a soup business during COVID-19 lockdowns – can load up their matzo balls with fragrant herbs and spices, but you can't make a silk purse out of a sow's ear, amirite? Why on earth would we want to eat, in non-Passover times, the whole or ground-up version of the bread of affliction our ancestors made in haste that TURNED OUT BAD? Matzo and matzo meal are gross. There. I said what I said. So here I am making my case. Justice for the forgotten and superior (with a little something called *flavour*) Jewish dumpling!

And, sadly, it has been forgotten. A quick survey of my city's restos revealed matzo ball soup galore, but no kreplach to be found, except at a super-trendy, Middle Eastern–inspired place, wowing with an Ottolenghi-ish, squash-filled kreplach main finished with pumpkin seed dukkah, but thoroughly unevocative of the meaty kreplach of my youth. My own ancestry is Ashkenazic; it turns out that one must schlep all the way out to a suburban deli for a delicious Ashkenazic-style bowl of kreplach soup – a shanda (disgrace), as my bubbies might have said.

So puzzling, as most big cities have a plethora of restos and shops dedicated to the filled dumplings of other cultures. But not so surprising once I start digging into kreplach history. Per Wikipedia, kreplach were traditionally made on three specific occasions, with the letters *K*, *R*, and *P* possibly signifying Yom Kippur, Rosh Hashanah, and Purim. Being the most secular of Jews, I never knew about this acronym. I had always just assumed that everyone made matzo balls (easy) because they were too lazy to make kreplach (complicated). The members of my family of origin all love food – my father supplied fish to many fine restaurants. But they do not love fiddly recipes. (Side note: as a very busy adult, I forgive you all.)

Of the dozens I came across, I love one particular explanation for the Yom Kippur association: kreplach, I learned on Chabad.org, were traditionally eaten before the Yom Kippur fast began, because the filling and its wrapper reminded us that we have inner as well as outer lives. During Yom Kippur we are expected to think about how we've acted over the previous year and the changes we intend to make to our behaviour going forward.

There are also a dozen explanations for the name besides the KRP acronym. For example, the *lach* could come from the

Yiddish word for *little*, and the *krep* might derive from the German *krepp*, meaning *crepe* (per Wikipedia again). Or not. And there are just as many explanations for the origin of *kreplach*: the Italian Jews' take on ravioli, Russian Jews' take on pelmeni, or Polish Jews' take on (mostly vegetarian) pierogies, Poland's national dish. My mother-in-law, born in Lublin, Poland, has both kreplach and pierogies in her repertoire.

Despite my strenuous defence of the neglected kreplach, I had never learned how to make them until the spring of 2022, when I felt obliged to do so, while writing this passionate defence of them. But I was hesitant. I learned how to make my maternal bubbie's fabulous, meat-filled knishes when she stopped cooking in the late 1980s; everybody else in my family of origin had refused, as knishes are even more fiddly than kreplach. In fact, when I told my bubbie about my first attempt, she laughed. She might as well have said, 'Aw, how cute that this little pisher thinks she can duplicate my fluffy, fried-to-golden-perfection Jewish delicacies.' She was right to laugh; I never could duplicate her knishes, though I gamely tried – and keep trying. But it's possible that her laugh, which haunts me still, precluded my attempt to make her kreplach, the ones I loved as a child.

Also, I had undoubtedly internalized the toxic notion of matzo ball supremacy.

Shortly after accepting the assignment to write this essay, I announced to my family that, henceforth, I would be making kreplach in addition to knishes. I looked up the kreplach recipe in that bible of Jewish cooking, Norene Gilletz's *Second Helpings, Please!*, a truly bizarre 1968 collection of classics mixed in with head-scratchers such as Lo-Cal Chicken – chicken marinated in low-calorie, bottled Italian salad dressing, then dipped in bread crumbs and baked. Gilletz's ingredient list was suspiciously sparse, so I abandoned it and asked my mostly-retired-from-cooking mother-in-law for her (delicious) kreplach recipe.

That one turned out to be from another Gilletz classic, *The Pleasures of Your Food Processor*. This recipe had a detailed list of ingredients and instructions for the dough but included even less direction about the filling than the *Second Helpings* volume. 'Prepare desired filling (cheese, leftover ground meat, chicken, or liver)' is all she wrote. Why do all the older books assume people already have a favourite way of preparing their favourite fillings for knishes or kreplach? We don't. That's why we need recipes!

Meanwhile, a search on the interwebs laid bare the fact that many modern-day cooks used prepared wonton wrappers, and, what's more, a nearby kosher grocery store sold frozen kreplach! I promptly bought wonton wrappers at the supermarket, as well as some frozen, ground-chicken-filled kreplach from the kosher grocer. I also found a bunch of detailed kreplach recipes online.

On the appointed evening, I enlisted my family in a kreplach taste-off, with the frozen chicken kreplach pitted against my own. I freestyled the filling. My mother-in-law told me she combines fried onions and ground chicken, so I did that, adding good amounts of dill and salt and pepper, as well as some fatty chicken broth, per Tori Avey's online recipe. Unlike my mother-in-law and Tori, I used the ready-made wonton wrappers. (Sue me.) And yay, my kreplach won the family A/B test.

Sadly, my loves are still, by and large, matzo ball people. But you can be sure that, having finally overcome my kreplach-making fears, I'll persist in trying to bring my family around to appreciating my favourite neglected dumpling!

The Sauce

New Year's Luck

Tatum Taylor Chaubal

In the dwindling hours of each New Year's Eve, I join the rush of panic shoppers before the supermarkets close for the holiday. It helps that I know my grocery list by rote – some sparkling wine and the key components of the next day's dinner: cornmeal, black-eyed peas, and cabbage. When I moved to Canada in 2012, I introduced my Indian wife to this tradition from Texas and the American South (the two are often conflated, though my parents and other Texans are vocal about the distinction). Black-eyed peas and cabbage are a recipe for prosperity and good fortune in the New Year, and cornmeal dumplings seal the meal.

I spent my first eighteen years in Houston, Texas, then gradually made my way northward, finally landing in Toronto. As a rare Texan in some senses – expatriated, queer, and a vegetarian! – it's taken me years to understand my relationship with my home state. Food is a significant factor; in Canada, my cravings for queso and fried okra and buttermilk pie stoke my pride. Over the years, my accent has faded, but I cling to the tastes of my childhood. I keep a stack of my parents' recipes in the kitchen, including cornmeal dumplings, though I don't need the instructions anymore. I'm not sure why I only ever cook peas, cabbage, and dumplings on

January 1; they make for a balanced dish, not complicated, and well-suited for any other day. But maybe I'm afraid to dull their New Year's magic.

Versions of this ritual are so firmly implanted in the southern U.S. that its roots may not be widely understood: for many practitioners, it has taken on the ambiguous urgency of unquestioned superstition. But despite this ubiquity, it's important to note that the tradition likely originates from Black American culture. Culinary historian Adrian Miller has said that the forced migration of enslaved Africans resulted in the intertwining of African and European foodways. Black-eyed peas are native to West Africa, and Black Americans transformed the combination of peas and greens into new customs. Some communities interpret the green stuff as collards, which made their way to the States from Northern Europe. Cabbage manifests a German influence, which reflects my own family background and that of many other Texans. According to the common lore, the peas look like pennies, the greens like dollar bills, and iterations of cornbread – in my case, dumplings – give the glimmer of gold.

Soaking overnight, the little pea coins swell quietly as fireworks crack the darkness and the old and new years meet. They spend the next day simmering with onion and jalapeno (I skip the pork that is also a typical ingredient). In the evening, while thick stacks of cabbage dollars sear on the side, I mix the cornmeal with flour, baking soda, buttermilk, butter, and a handful of green onion. Then I drop pecan-sized balls of cornbread dough to steam in a closed pot, right on top of the black-eyed peas. After a few moments, I can't resist taking a peek – the peas bubbling up like champagne – then quickly shut the lid. Eight or nine minutes later, I remove the lid again, and the veil of vapour dissipates to reveal the dumplings, puffed up to double their pre-steamed size, the peas now fully covered by hillocks of gold flecked with green. Dished out, they beg to be eaten with a dash of hot sauce or, if you're like my wife, a deluge of it.

Once, we topped each dumpling with a spoonful of 'chow-chow,' a relish consisting of various pickled vegetables. In keeping with the traditional lucky ingredients, I prefer a dominant note of cabbage; in fact, the condiment's name is thought to derive from the French word for cabbage – *chou*. We bought a jar specifically for this purpose while in Virginia for our wedding in 2018, from an Amish woman who couldn't believe we didn't have chowchow in Canada (though I've heard the Maritimes have their own version). 'I'd die without my chow-chow,' she told us earnestly. We ate that year's version with particular – forgive me – relish.

On December 31, 2021, we bought the ingredients to mark our second (or third?) New Year's in a global pandemic. When I called my parents with 2022 greetings, they told me they were finally forgoing the tradition: 'It doesn't seem to have done much for anyone in the fortune department lately.' They ate stuffed peppers instead.

But fortune is relative, and I wasn't taking any risks. If the world was spinning askew in spite of the yearly peas, cabbage, and dumplings, I couldn't imagine what fate awaited us if we skipped the meal. With any luck, I'll never know.

Gnocchi Love

Domenica Marchetti

My parents met on a blind date in New York City, but it was gnocchi that cemented their relationship. Early in their dating life, my mom decided to make dinner for her new beau. The scene is 1950s Manhattan. Picture her: outgoing, stylish, hour-glass shape, newly arrived from Italy, and determined to chart her own course. Him: recently graduated from Brown University with a degree in chemical engineering; slim, with dark wavy hair and dark eyes, quiet but with a dry sense of humour.

On the day in question, armed with potatoes, flour, and a recipe, she set about to making a dish she had enjoyed many times growing up in Abruzzo but had never made herself: gnocchi al sugo (gnocchi with tomato sauce). She boiled the potatoes and riced them, measured out the flour, and kneaded the two together. The mixture was sticky, so she added more flour. The more my mom kneaded, the stickier it became. Yet she kept kneading and adding more flour until she had to go to the store for more. When her date arrived, my mom was still trying to wrangle the gooey lump into a workable dough. Finally, in a moment of supreme frustration, she lifted the entire mass and heaved it at the wall. My parents had dinner out that night. But my mom learned a valuable lesson: if you are impatient, gnocchi will defeat you.

It's true: they are notoriously fussy to make. What's more, just because you've made them successfully once doesn't mean you will be successful the next time. All sorts of variables can affect the outcome, from the type of potato you use to how humid it is in your kitchen. Even the name *gnocchi* invites confusion. I've been referring to classic potato gnocchi here, but did you know there are dozens of types of Italian dumplings and dumpling-like pastas that go by the name *gnocchi*? Still others are part of the gnocchi family but go by different names entirely. Gnocchi are as varied and regional (and confounding) as Italian cuisine itself and, consequently, can be made with a spectrum of ingredients: bread, flour, ground chestnuts, polenta, ricotta, potato, and pumpkin among them. (And yes, *gnocchi* is plural, just like *biscotti* and *cannoli*; the singular term is *gnocco*.)

Over the years I have 'collected' (by which I mean eaten) all sorts of gnocchi. Some I've encountered at restaurants and private homes while travelling around Italy; others I've made in my kitchen, using as my source the pile of Italian cookbooks passed down to me from my mom. Here, for your enjoyment, is a short list of favourites:

Canederli: These dumplings, nearly the size of tennis balls, come from Alto Adige, on Italy's border with Austria (note the similarity between the word *canederli* and the German *knodel*). Finely chopped speck (smoked prosciutto) is usually added to the bread mixture, though sometimes it's blanched greens or even radicchio. Despite their hefty appearance, canederli are surprisingly light. They are served either in hot broth or tossed with melted butter and cheese.

Gnocchi di Castagne: Chestnuts grow in abundance in the wooded hills of Liguria, north of the Italian Riviera, and have long been an important source of nutrition for the region. So it makes sense that they would make their way into gnocchi, in the form of chestnut flour. The nuts are slowly roasted, over a period of weeks, then ground to produce a slightly bitter, slightly sweet flour, tinged with smoke. It's the flour that gives these gnocchi their beguiling flavour. They are typically served with a light cream sauce so the smoky sweetness of the chestnut flour comes through.

Raviole della Valvaraita: Local to Piemonte's Cuneo province, these spindle-shaped gnocchi are made with flour, potatoes, and a soft cheese called tomino di Melle, though robiola can be substituted. They are served with warmed cream, fresh alpine butter, and Parmigiano cheese, a testament to the region's dairy supremacy.

Pisarei e Faśö: Unlike the oversized canederli, these bread-crumb-and-egg gnocchi from Emilia-Romagna are mini – about the size of a bean. Appropriately, they are served in a sauce of borlotti beans cooked with tomatoes, lard, and onion.

Malfatti: Also called gnudi, these tender, walnut-sized spinach-and-ricotta dumplings are a specialty of Tuscany. *Malfatti* translates to poorly made, and *gnudi* to nude. Both names refer to the fact that these dumplings are, essentially, spinach-and-cheese ravioli without their pasta jackets. They are simply coated in flour, boiled in water, and dressed with tomato sauce or melted butter and sage.

Ndunderi: Dating to Roman times, these plump dumplings from the Amalfi Coast were once made with fresh, soft cheese curd mixed with flour. The modern iteration combines fresh ricotta with egg yolks and flour and, in some versions, potatoes. They are less fluffy than classic potato gnocchi and stand up well to a classic southern-style pork-and-sausage ragù.

Gnocchi alla Romana: Also known as gnocchi di semolina, these are made by cooking semolina in milk, then combining the thick mixture with butter and eggs. The dense batter is spread out to cool, then cut into rounds or diamonds, layered in a dish, and baked, gratin-style, with Parmigiano cheese. Gnocchi alla Romana is still a beloved dish at many trattorias in and around Rome.

Gnocchi de Susini: Fruit-filled gnocchi from Trieste have a decidedly Eastern European aspect, which makes sense given the city's proximity to Slovenia and Croatia. Potato dough is wrapped around softened prunes or dried apricots and formed into balls. As with other gnocchi, these are boiled in water. But rather than a savoury sauce, they are tossed with bread crumbs sautéed in butter, sugar, and cinnamon.

This is by no means a complete list, but it gives you an idea of the delicious assortment that exists within the world of gnocchi. As for the word itself, the origin is hazy, but it is thought to derive from either *nocca* (knuckle), *nodo* (knot), or *noce* (walnut). According to Gambero Rosso, one of Italy's leading food media companies, the first references date back to fifteenth-century Renaissance-era chefs, who described dumplings made by mixing flour, bread crumbs, hot water, and eggs. The dough was cut into nuggets, and these were rolled along the backside of a grater to create texture, a method still used today. The gnocchi were dressed in butter, cheese, and spices.

Potato gnocchi date to the sixteenth or seventeenth century, after the tuber had been introduced to Europe by Spanish explorers returning from South America. Pellegrino Artusi, a Florentine silk merchant and noted nineteenth-century gastronome, included a recipe in his seminal book, *La Scienza in Cucina e l'Arte di Mangiar Bene* (*Science in the Kitchen and the Art of Eating Well*). Published in 1891, it was the first book of Italian regional recipes written in the common Italian language and aimed at an emerging middle class. Artusi's recipe for potato gnocchi is still considered a blueprint. It contains just two ingredients – 'mealy' potatoes and flour, as well as an anecdotal warning that underscores just how tricky this recipe can be to properly execute: 'The flour serves to bind the gnocchi and thus forestall the experience of a lady who, in my presence, stirred the pot and came up with nothing at all; the gnocchi had disappeared … [They] were made with too little flour and dissolved upon coming into contact with the boiling water.'

Watching a batch of handmade gnocchi dissolve into goo is a special kind of heartache (I speak from experience). One way to steer clear of this soul-crushing disaster is to add an egg or an egg yolk to the dough, which helps to bind the gnocchi without making them stodgy. Hardliners view this method as a cop-out, but I don't. I find the egg gives gnocchi just enough body without sacrificing lightness.

The egg-or-no-egg debate is just one of many that divide cooks about proper gnocchi techniques. Most of the others have to do with the potatoes: What type should you use? Should you boil or bake them? Should you mash or rice? Do you mix the dough while the potatoes are still hot or do you let them cool first?

The best way to answer these questions, of course, is to roll up your sleeves and start making gnocchi. That's what my mom did, for while she could be impatient, she was also stubborn and could not abide a kitchen fail. By the time I came along, she was turning out beautifully tender, pillowy gnocchi, and her recipe has served as my blueprint since I started making them nearly two decades ago (sorry, Signor Artusi!). Her secret, by the way, was not just the type of potatoes she used (a mix of baking and yellow potatoes) and the addition of an egg, but also a splash of grappa added to the dough. She claimed it kept the gnocchi light and gave them a flavour boost, but I believe she did it more as a gesture of affection to my grappa-loving dad.

GNOCCHI DI PATATE

First, some tips to keep in mind when making gnocchi:

1. Use old, floury potatoes. Typically, this means baking potatoes, which are drier than yellow or red potatoes. However, mature yellow potatoes also work well and have more flavour than baking potatoes. To get the best of both, use a mix.
2. Boil, don't bake, your potatoes. It's true that baking yields 'drier' potatoes, but often they are too dry to turn into a workable dough. Boil the potatoes whole in their skins until they are completely tender, so you don't have any hard bits in your gnocchi.
3. Rice the potatoes rather than mash them. This keeps them fluffy. Rice them onto a floured surface while they are still hot so steam and moisture can escape.
4. A metal or plastic bench scraper is useful to bring the dough together without overhandling it, and for cutting the gnocchi.
5. Most people worry that their gnocchi will be tough. This is a valid concern, so make sure you don't incorporate too much flour or overknead the dough. However, the opposite problem can also occur, as Artusi mentioned: if you don't add enough flour, your gnocchi will dissolve. It can take a few tries to find the right balance. Knead with a light hand, but don't be afraid to handle the dough.
6. Before you roll out all your gnocchi, test a small batch: Bring a small pot of water to a boil and slide in a few gnocchi. They cook quickly and will bob to the surface in less than a minute. If they dissolve partially or

completely, you need more flour; knead a little more into the dough and test again before shaping the rest.

7. Shape the gnocchi as soon as the dough is mixed. Unlike pasta dough, gnocchi dough does not benefit from a rest. The shaped gnocchi also should not sit out for too long before being cooked – a few hours at most.

8. Be patient. Mastering gnocchi takes practice. Are they worth it? Absolutely. There's a reason a dish featuring nothing but potatoes and flour, and maybe a little egg, has stuck around for five centuries.

INGREDIENTS

for 4 to 6 servings

2 lbs (900 g) mature potatoes, preferably a mix of Yukon Gold and baking potatoes

Salt

2¼ cups (300 g) unbleached all-purpose flour, plus more as needed

1 large egg, at room temperature

1 Tbsp grappa or vodka (optional)

Tomato sauce, ragù, or pesto, for serving

Freshly grated Parmigiano cheese, for serving

INSTRUCTIONS

1. Wash the potatoes and put them in a large pot with water to cover by 2 inches. Salt the water generously and bring to a boil over medium-high heat. Boil for 25 minutes or until the potatoes are completely tender. Drain in a colander set in the sink. As soon as they are cool enough to handle, peel them, cut them into quarters, and pass them through a potato ricer onto a clean, flour-dusted work surface, spreading them into a

shallow mound. Make a well in the centre, then let the potatoes cool for a few minutes.

2. Sprinkle 2 cups flour all around the perimeter of the potatoes. Break the egg into the well, then add the grappa. Using a fork, beat the egg and begin to incorporate the potatoes. Keep mixing, eventually incorporating the flour around the perimeter as well. A dough scraper comes in handy here to help bring the mixture together without overworking it. Switch to your hands and lightly knead the mixture into a soft ball of dough. It should feel pliant, slightly tacky, and somewhat 'shaggy' or rough rather than smooth. If the dough is too soft and sticky to handle, incorporate another handful or two of flour. This is tricky, as you don't want to overwork the dough or add too much flour. On the other hand, if you don't add enough flour, your gnocchi risk dissolving when you cook them. After you've made gnocchi a few times, you will get a feel for the correct texture of the dough. Cover the dough with a bowl or clean towel and scrape away any stuck bits from the work surface.

3. Line two rimmed baking sheets with clean kitchen towels (or cover a table with a clean tablecloth) and dust with flour. Set aside. Have a ridged gnocchi board or a fork at the ready. Sprinkle a little flour onto your work surface. Slice off a piece of dough about the size of a tangerine. Using your palms, roll out the dough into a rope about the thickness of your finger (¾ inch). Use a knife or the dough scraper to cut the rope into ¾-inch to 1-inch nuggets. Roll the nuggets, one at a time, down the gnocchi board or the tines of the fork, using your thumb or a finger to lightly propel it downward and, at the same time, create a small groove. When you are done, you should have the

groove from your finger on one side of the nuggets and the ridges from the board or fork on the other side. Transfer your gnocchi to the baking sheets or tablecloth as you work, making sure they are not touching, or they will clump together. Flour your workspace and hands as needed to prevent the gnocchi from sticking.

4. Before continuing, test-cook a few gnocchi: bring a small pot of salted water to a boil and slide in 4 or 5 gnocchi; they should bob to the surface within a minute. Let them cook briefly (taste one to make sure there is no raw flour taste), then use a spider or slotted spoon to transfer them to a bowl. If they start to 'dissolve' into goo in the water, you need to add more flour to the dough. Sprinkle a handful of flour on top of the mass and quickly but gently work it in before rolling out more gnocchi. Test again if necessary. Once all the gnocchi are shaped, let them sit, uncovered, for about 30 minutes to develop a light 'skin'; this will keep them from sticking to one another when dropped into boiling water. Then cover them with a clean kitchen towel.

5. To cook the gnocchi, bring a large pot of water to a rolling boil and salt it generously. Carefully drop in the gnocchi, in batches, to avoid overcrowding the pot. Within 30 to 45 seconds, the gnocchi will begin to float to the surface. Taste one; it should be soft and fluffy but cooked throughout, with no residual flour taste. Using a spider or slotted spoon, transfer the gnocchi to a warmed serving bowl or platter and gently toss with a little sauce – fresh tomato sauce, sausage ragù, and pesto are my favourite sauces for gnocchi. Continue until all the gnocchi are cooked. Toss gently with more sauce, sprinkle with Parmigiano cheese, and serve.

The Perogy Bees of the Prairies

Julie Van Rosendaal

Perogies – though there are many spellings, I default to the one used by Baba's Homestyle Perogies in Saskatoon, where you can get a plate of fried perogies with onions and mushroom-dill sauce at the country's only perogy drive-thru – are not part of my family history. We didn't even eat frozen Cheemos for dinner at my house. But growing up on the Prairies, I've shared my life with plenty of Ukrainian and Polish friends, and as such have happily eaten far more than my share. Perogies are a staple here, having arrived with waves of Eastern European immigrants in the late nineteenth and early twentieth centuries. An estimated 150,000 Ukrainians settled in Western Canada between 1891 and 1914, the majority seeking out farmland in Manitoba, Saskatchewan, and Alberta, where the government promoted cheap land in order to populate their wide-open spaces.

These newly established communities continued to grow after World Wars I and II, fuelled by the wheat, potatoes, onions, and cabbage that grew in abundance here. Hearty dumplings were well-suited to farm work and long Canadian winters. But beyond their economy, practicality, and deliciousness, they were social building blocks, humble catalysts that brought communities of women together to roll, fill, and pinch in an effort to raise enough money to feed a wedding party, fund a community project, or repair a church.

I dreamed of being part of a perogy bee – a gathering of perogy pinchers channelling generations of experience through their fingers – for decades, before I was finally invited to one, and it was all I imagined it would be: long tables covered in plastic, scattered with flour and balls of dough, rolling pins and bowls of mashed potato. Deft hands working with as much speed and precision as any machine, turning out piles of perogies while catching up on the who and what. Perogy bees were the community water cooler, the social media of generations past.

When you think about it, a perogy is the edible embodiment of comfort – a literal pillow filled with downy potatoes and (if you're lucky) cheese. People ask if I prefer sweet or savoury, and I'm in neither camp: I'm crispy-chewy or crunchy-soft, a combination of textures that tends to show up in so many of my favourite things. As I don't have Eastern European roots, I sought out a perogy recipe via my friend Cheryl, who learned from her baba Nettie. She taught me how she did it in her own kitchen one weekend, her young daughters at our side. I use Nettie's technique now: roll the warm dough into a thick rope, cut it into pieces, and roll each piece into a circle to fill, eliminating scraps.

I am, however, particular about how I cook my perogies: boiled and then tossed via slotted spoon into the hot skillet that has just caramelized more onions than I think I'll need, to develop a crisp outer crust to contrast with the chewy dough and soft interior. Topping them with sour cream while they're still hot, allowing the cream to melt slightly into the crevices – I can think of few better things to eat.

I make perogies in true dumpling tradition – as a way to use up leftovers, particularly after a celebratory dinner for which I made far too many potatoes. Cold roasted veg, gravy, and scraps from yesterday's meal can be chopped and stuffed into a perogy, which means they also win points as a means of reducing food waste. And while perogy bees are fewer and further between than they once were, there's no reason you can't invite a few friends over and have your own, many hands making light work of the assembly as you catch up and fill each other's freezers with some comfort food for another day.

During the first year of the pandemic, I boosted my Zoom account one weekend to accommodate over three hundred friends (and some of their friends and relatives) for a virtual perogy bee. We spent a Saturday afternoon channelling our worries into dinner, each of us rolling, filling, and pinching perogies in our own kitchens, comforted by the sight of one another's faces and the sound of our voices. The surplus we made and froze were door-dropped – one of the best traditions to emerge over the past few years – on the porches and steps of neighbours.

In early 2022, when Russia invaded Ukraine, communities around the world responded by raising funds by any means they could, and often it was by gathering in kitchens and making perogies. In the community of Vegreville, just east of Edmonton, volunteers made, boiled, and served about twelve thousand perogies to around a thousand dinner guests. In the kitchens of similar community halls and church basements across Canada, perogies were once again a means of connection, a way to show love and support to those near and far. Food provides comfort in more ways than just the eating – it's also the gathering, the socializing, and the feeling of being cared for that comes from having someone feed you.

SASKATOON PEROGIES

Though most of us think of potatoes, onions, and cheese when it comes to perogies, they can also be dessert and are often stuffed with sour cherries or saskatoons. Freeze perogies in a single layer on a baking sheet, then transfer to zip-lock bags to store. Boil directly from frozen. If you like, brown well-drained boiled perogies in a hot pan with butter until crisp and golden; dribble the remaining butter from the pan overtop.

DOUGH
3 cups all-purpose flour
1 tsp salt
¾ cup milk
1 large egg
2 Tbsp canola oil
⅓–½ cup hot water

FILLING
½ cup sugar
1 Tbsp all-purpose flour
2 cups fresh or frozen saskatoons or pitted sour cherries
Butter, for cooking
Sour cream, for serving

Dough: In a large bowl, stir together the flour and salt. In a small bowl, stir together the milk, egg, and oil; add to the flour mixture and stir until you have a shaggy mixture. Add the water and stir until you have a soft, tacky dough. Knead about 10 times, cover with a towel, and let rest for 20 minutes.

Filling: Combine the sugar and flour; stir in the saskatoons.

Roll out the dough about ⅛-inch thick and cut into 3-inch rounds. Fill with a spoonful of the saskatoon mixture, fold over the dough to cover, and pinch the edges together to seal. In a large pot of lightly salted water, boil perogies in batches; once they float to the top, boil for another minute, then transfer to a dish with a slotted spoon. Serve with sour cream. Makes about 3 dozen.

If Life Is a Bowl of Cherries, Why am I Eating Matzo Ball Soup?

(With apologies to Erma Bombeck)

Amy Rosen

'Who made these? They're dry.'
'They're definitely not as good as yours.'
'Quiet, she'll hear.'
'If we don't say anything, how will she learn?'
                    – Overheard at every High Holiday meal

You can enjoy chicken soup in as many ways as you can fill a pot. You can have pho, Italian wedding, tom kha gai, or even Campbell's chicken noodle soup. But until I see a big, fluffy matzo ball bobbing in broth, your soup means nothing to me. Once ball hits bowl, however, this becomes *my* business. Memories of Shabbos dinners come flooding back like the Red Sea drowning Pharaoh's army. And I smile, recalling the annual moment when I snap my Haggadah shut and can finally begin eating the Seder meal. Then it starts, just like it always does, with that familiar taste – perhaps *the* most familiar taste.

Matzo balls are the iconic Jewish recipe. People may not know a single Jew or a single thing about Judaism, but most will know what matzo balls look and taste like. And they usually want to know a little bit more about the Jewish culture once they've tried them. (They really are that good!) So, how is it that a simple bowl of chicken broth, golden-hued from chicken fat, flecked with dill, and festooned with fluffy matzo balls, is all things to all people? How did this delicious dumpling come to be?

Let's explore how matzo ball soup – a six-ingredient wonder – became the most important recipe to generations of Jews.

Germans, Alsatians, and Austrians used to make dumplings using the leftover crumbs from the matzo bread they would buy at their local nineteenth-century bakeries. Back then, these dumplings were known as knoedel. When Jews moved to Poland, they called them knaidlach, and that's what my family calls them too.

While researching the genesis of the matzo ball, I came across a story in *Time* magazine: 'In 1838, a Frenchman named Isaac Singer invented a matzo-dough-rolling machine that cut down on the dough's prep time and made mass production possible,' the article said. But as we all know, changes to three-thousand-year-old religious traditions don't come easy, and Singer's invention wasn't eagerly embraced by the nineteenth-century Jewish authorities.

Fast-forward to 1888. A Lithuanian immigrant named Dov Behr, who later changed his surname to Manischewitz, opened the world's first matzo-making factory in Cincinnati, Ohio. He named his factory the B. Manischewitz Company and developed a fully automated method for matzo making. Said *Time*: 'Manischewitz endured some controversy for his use of machines, but after he spent 13 years studying the Talmud in Jerusalem, even the most hardened traditionalists eventually considered him an acceptable authority on matzo.' (Jews!)

In the 1930s, Manischewitz began packaging what is now known as matzo ball mix, though back then they called these cooked dumplings 'Alsatian feathery balls.' Nobody can say for certain who changed the name to matzo balls, but I think I speak for everyone when I say we are forever grateful.

So, who likes matzo balls these days? Well, David Beckham for one. I didn't realize Beckham had Jewish heritage (even though his name is David) until I heard him on the *River Cafe Table 4* podcast with Ruth Rogers, during which the soccer star discussed spending Shabbos dinners at his Jewish grandfather's house. 'So, every Saturday when we'd turn up,' he said, 'my gran would have this most amazing chicken noodle soup with the matzo meal dumplings. That's what I was brought up on.' Even though he was raised in a secular household, Beckham said he identifies as 'half-Jewish.' I can't help but wonder how many more Jewish kids would be playing soccer today if they had known he was one of us.

Another matzo-ball-loving Jew is Lily, my ten-year-old niece, who likes them more than just about anyone I know. Except, perhaps, for her younger sister Ivy. I ask Lily why she loves matzo ball soup so much.

'It's very flavourful and has a lot of moisture,' she says.

'The soup has moisture?'

'The matzo balls do.'

'Would you eat chicken soup without matzo balls?'

'No.'

'Why not?'

'There's no point.'

I saw a meme recently that simply said, 'When to eat matzo ball soup,' followed by six illustrations of the same bowl of matzo ball soup, with captions like 'Have a cold,' 'Going through a bad breakup,' or 'Therapist on vacation.' As with any successful meme, it's funny because it's true.

If I have a bowl of commercially made chicken noodle soup, it doesn't heal what ails me or remind me of matzo ball soup, even though most of the ingredients are the same. For, while it may be chicken soup in name and thus inherently warming, it doesn't bring me back to anywhere.

Many recipes evoke specific memories. But matzo balls evoke *recurring* memories. Any time Jews gather to celebrate, or to mourn, we have matzo ball soup with the people with whom we are most ourselves. Whoever you are, surly teen, new university student, adorable toddler, as soon as a bowl of matzo ball soup is involved, something is triggered – a smile, a longing, or even naptime. When it comes to matzo balls, context is everything.

My friend Dana, who keeps a kosher home and celebrates Shabbos dinner each week, says when her family is sitting down to have matzo ball soup, they're generally at their best. 'We're at our happiest because it's not a rushed Wednesday night in the throes of life,' she explains. 'It's a welcome pause.' Nobody has ever enjoyed a hot bowl of matzo ball soup on the run. Case closed. It's for Friday nights when it's calm, when we're saying prayers over the Shabbos candles, the wine, and especially the challah. When we're catching up with family and friends while trying to be good Jews.

'My parents were just in town visiting,' says Dana, 'And the first thing my mom did was make chicken soup and matzo balls. My kids like hers better than mine. I tell them that's okay, because one day your kids will think my matzo balls are the best.' It's officially a thing: my bubbie Fran's matzo ball soup was legendary, and my mom's grandchildren all think her matzo ball soup is the best. While all Jewish grandmothers can't possibly lay claim to the world's best matzo ball soup, they've all got a secret ingredient that the rest of us don't: that special feeling of a bubbie's love.

So, the soup is one thing – fortified with chicken schmaltz, schmaltzy love – and just the right amount of fresh dill. But the matzo balls are a bit of a riddle. Since so many of us use the exact same boxed mix from the B. Manischewitz Company, how on earth can there be this never-ending discussion over who makes the best matzo balls? If you listen around the Rosh Hashanah dinner table, shouts of 'Give 'em to me fluffy!' and 'Only sinkers for me!' can often be heard.

Well, I'm here to tell you that the person who makes the world's best matzo balls is not up for debate. Because the world's best matzo balls are the ones that most closely resemble the ones you grew up with. (It was you, all along!) Memories, after all, make everything perfect.

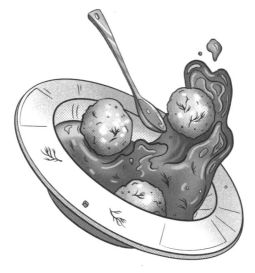

MATZO BALLS

You probably want to make matzo balls now. Here's my easy recipe. In a large bowl, stir together 4 beaten eggs, 1 cup matzo meal, 2 tablespoons vegetable oil, 1½ teaspoons salt, ¼ teaspoon freshly ground pepper, 2 tablespoons minced fresh parsley, and 1 teaspoon of baking powder. Add ¼ cup of soda water and mix well. Cover and refrigerate for at least 30 minutes.

Fill a large pot with salted water and bring to a boil, then lower to a simmer. Working gently, with wet or oiled hands, form the matzo mix into walnut-sized balls, dropping them into the water as you go. When all the matzo balls are in the water, cover the pot and gently simmer for 35 to 40 minutes, or until cooked through and soft. Remove from water with a slotted spoon and serve in chicken soup. You can also make them a day in advance and keep them covered in the fridge, warming them up in the soup. Makes about 12 matzo balls.

What's in a Name? The Jamaican Patty Controversy

Cheryl Thompson

M y parents are Jamaican and immigrated to Canada in the mid-1960s. When I was a child growing up in Toronto, my mother cooked Jamaican food, but she also prepared mainstream dishes, like spaghetti. It wasn't until I attended public school that I realized that not all children ate cooked fish with 'ground provisions' (potatoes, yams, boiled banana, and other root vegetables typical of Jamaican cuisine) for breakfast. That culinary custom was distinctly Caribbean.

When I was twenty-seven, I moved out of my parents' house and relocated to an apartment in the city. I had to prepare my own meals for the first time in my life. While I had cooked when I lived at home, I never dared prepare Jamaican food. That was my mother's domain, and her cooking was so good, I didn't presume to step into her territory. But after I moved out, she gave me a Jamaican cookbook in case I wanted to keep up the tradition of cooking foods from our ancestral homeland. That book, *Traditional Jamaican Cookery*, written by food historian Norma Benghiat and published in 1985, is a literal how-to for every Jamaican dish you can think of, from curry chicken to oxtail, ackee and salt fish (the country's national dish), stew peas and rice (my personal favourite). The book also contains a recipe for patties, and specifically the beef patty.

I love spicy beef patties and eat them often. A Jamaican beef patty contains a meat filling seasoned with herbs and spices and encased in a semi-hard pastry that is baked until it's a golden yellow colour. I usually buy my patties from a pastry shop in the Bathurst subway station in Toronto. Patties have become Jamaican comfort food. While beef is the original flavour, patties are now sold in many varieties – jerk, saltfish, ackee and saltfish, and shrimp. With its delicious combination of spices encased in a light pastry, it is perfect for a snack or light meal. But, like most cuisines born of Black communities, it has a complicated history that intersects with colonialism and the Western world.

Jamaica, 383 kilometres south of Cuba and 537 kilometres west of Haiti and the Dominican Republic, was first colonized by Spain in the fifteenth century. Cities such as Port Antonio and Ocho Rios, on the northeast coast, and Spanish Town, the capital and largest town in the parish of St. Catherine, point to the legacy of Spanish colonial rule on the island.

In 1655, Jamaica was colonized by the British as they expanded their conquest of Caribbean islands. Between the sixteenth and nineteenth centuries, Portuguese Jews settled on the island, after fleeing Spain following the Inquisition. They brought with them Spanish recipes, such as pea and bean dishes, which are very similar to the foods prepared by the Sephardic Jews in the Middle East, according to Benghiat. Chinese and Indian immigrants also arrived in Jamaica during the nineteenth and early twentieth centuries, bringing with them herbs, spices, and culinary dishes unique to their homelands.

Following the Haitian Revolution in 1789, many white and Black people who had been planters, artisans, printers, blacksmiths, and tailors arrived in Jamaica, bringing vegetables known as 'leggins' (a word possibly derived from *legumes*). As Benghiat writes, when the 'French émigrés from Haiti … arrived during the eighteenth century [they] are said to have brought with them the recipe for what has become a national favourite – patties.'

When the first Africans were brought to the island by the Spanish, and then later by the British, the most dominant ethnic groups were the Ashanti and Fante peoples (from present-day Ghana), as well as the Yoruba peoples (from present-day Nigeria, Benin, and Togo) and Ibo (from present-day Cameroon, Gabon, and Equatorial Guinea).

Over time, the African foods indigenous to these countries combined with dishes imported by previous immigrants to Jamaica. They all became part of the country's staple foods.

One example of this process of cross-fertilization is ackee and saltfish. Ackee, which is native to Ghana, was brought to the island, probably on a slave ship, from the West African country sometime in the mid-1700s. Saltfish, on the other hand, originated in Northern Europe and Maritime Canada. As a result of triangular slave trade between Britain, West Africa, and the Caribbean and North American colonies in the eighteenth and nineteenth centuries, large quantities of salted cod from Nova Scotia were traded for rum, sugar, and molasses, and in the process landed in Jamaica, where enslaved Africans combined it with ackee, producing the dish now known as ackee and saltfish. In 1962, when Jamaica declared its independence, ackee and saltfish became the country's national dish.

Africans in Jamaica cultivated their own cuisine, which included provisions such as yams, pigeon (gungo) peas, okra, callaloo, corn, cocoa, coffee, hot peppers, pimentos, pumpkins, and ackees – ingredients that can be found in most Jamaican foods, including the patty.

'The patty's journey to fruition is as varied as Jamaica's history,' writes Bryan Washington in the *New York Times Magazine*. 'And while the dish has (mostly) avoided the Americanized "elevation" of so many immigrant cuisines, you'll find beef patties in restaurants, across bar tops and behind convenience-shop counters wherever the Caribbean diaspora has made a home.'

In Canada, however, the patty had to resist Canadianization. In 1985, the Canadian government sought to force Jamaican patty shops in Toronto to rename the beef patty because, according to the bureaucratic definition of 'beef patty' used by the Canadian Meat Inspection Act, any item sold as a 'patty' could only contain meat (fresh or cooked), salt, seasonings, and flavour enhancers and was destined to go in a hamburger bun. A beef patty, according to the federal government's definition, 'could not contain fillers like breadcrumbs, oats, or whatever is stuffed into fast-food tacos. It could not be enclosed in dough or pastry.'

In what became known as the 'Patty Wars,' Jamaican vendors in the city refused to change the patty's name, defending their right to maintain the integrity of a beloved cultural food. The main vendor targeted by the government's probe, Michael Davidson, was manager of his family's bakery, Kensington Patty Palace, which opened in the 1970s when his parents immigrated to Canada. The 2022 CBC documentary *Patty vs. Patty* retells the case. One day, when Davidson's parents were away on vacation in Jamaica, he received a visit from a Canadian food inspector who demanded that he and eight other patty vendors rename their product. If they did not comply, they would be fined $5,000. Compliance included changing not only the patty's name but also their menus, packaging, and store signs.

Jamaican government officials intervened to support the local vendors while the Jamaican community flooded the Jamaican consulate in Toronto with calls of concern about the racist undertone of the regulation. In the face of mounting negative publicity, the federal government caved, and vendors were allowed to continue calling a patty a patty, but with one caveat – they had to amend their descriptions to include the adjective 'Jamaican.' They could not simply call this dish a 'beef patty.'

While the ordeal was horrible, some good came from it. Every February, to celebrate the victory, a patty festival is held in Toronto, an event that helps promote one of Jamaica's most prized dishes while also introducing it to people who have yet to enjoy this tasty delight.

Wherever there is a Jamaican diasporic community – from Toronto to New York, Philadelphia to Miami, Brixton to Birmingham – patties are the street food of choice. Patties are a delicacy because of the food's cultural specificity – they are unique to Jamaica. I've been eating them my entire life. In fact, if there is one thing I consider distinctively Jamaican, after reggae music, it's the patty. While my mother never made patties at home – her specialty was curry goat – whenever we meet up, eating a spicy patty together from Bathurst station connects us to each other, but also to our ancestral home.

The (Cornish) Pasty Wars

John Lorinc

By any journalistic measure, it was a headline writer's dream come true.

'Humble Pie? Cornish Pasty Set to Join the Upper Crust.'

'Cornish Pasties Are No One's Patsies.'

'Cornish Pasty Wins Battle Against Half-Baked Imitations.'

The occasion for all this punning had to do with the culmination, in October 2010, of a decade-long battle by a cartel of Cornwall-based food processors to secure 'protected geographical indication' status from the European Union. The designation ensures that any product marketed as a Cornish pasty (pronounced with a soft *a*) must be made in Cornwall, a rugged coastal region of South West England. Similar protections have been provided to a range of other food products, such as Parma ham and Kentish ale, as well as spirits, such as Kentucky bourbon, which must be distilled within the state, or champagne, which can be marketed under that name only if it's made with grapes from the Champagne region of France.

Cornish pasties, also known as 'oggies,' are D-shaped pockets of baked dough encasing a filling that consists of beef, potatoes, turnips, and onions, and seasoned with salt and pepper. The crust is a rich brownish yellow, flaky yet firm. The outer edge is rimmed with a thick braid of dough, about which more later.

The campaign had been initiated by a small Cornwall bakery founded in 1998. As the *Economist* explained, 'The pasty's unlikely conquest of Britain has been spearheaded by the West Cornwall Pasty Company. Its strategy was to eschew the crowded Cornish market, instead selling pasties to the rest of the country. It worked; several years of break-neck growth followed. In 2007 the founders sold the firm to Gresham, a private equity house, for £40m.'

But spokespeople for the Cornish pasty industry, which claims to employ tens of thousands of people, cast the EU's decision in terms far grander than a savvy business strategy.

'By guaranteeing the quality of the Cornish pasty, we are helping to protect our British food legacy,' Alan Adler, chair of the Cornish Pasty Association (CPA), told the *Daily Telegraph*. 'We lag far behind other European countries, such as France and Italy, that have hundreds of food products protected, and it's important that we value our foods just as much.'

Other players, however, were less than enthusiastic about this turn, with supermarkets and producers of competing pasty-like products complaining that they'd been elbowed aside. As one Devon-based Cornish pasty manufacturer told the *Telegraph*, the EU bureaucrats who issued the edict could 'go to hell.'

The fact that such a vitriolic response came from a Devon-based firm is not incidental and has to do with more than just the commercial interests involved. As the CPA's push for special status gained momentum, a geyser of atmospheric details about the history of the pasty, including its geograph-ical origins, erupted.

Some claimed that pasties had originated in Devon, the region just east of Cornwall. (The two counties are separated by the River Tamar.) Others dug up evidence purporting to show that the pasty had Welsh roots, a truly alarming detail (if you're English). 'It's the latest in a long series of battles between Wales and England,' according to the *Western Mail*, a Welsh media outfit based in Cardiff. 'The snack is commonly associated with Cornwall, but another pretty seaside county has now laid claim to the history of the meat-and-pastry treat – Pembrokeshire.' The article cited local historians who claimed to have found evidence of pasties filled with lamb, leeks, and currants that were served to labourers working on a Pembrokeshire cathedral in 1181.

The search for the pasty's culinary antecedents widened to include other less geographically specific tidbits, such as a reference in a letter by Jane Seymour, Henry VIII's third wife. The *Western Mail* also reported on a pasty allusion in Shakespeare, who, the paper noted, 'referred to pasties in *All's Well That Ends Well*, in which the character Parolles says: "I will confess to what I know without constraint: if ye pinch me like a pasty, I can say no more."'

While these details were interesting and added some heat to the debate, the more relevant historical explanation involves that thick braid of crust and its original purpose – a story that begins, strangely enough, with Cornwall's centuries-old tin and copper mining industry. Seams of these valuable metals ran deep below Cornwall's Atlantic cliffs, which came to be dotted with mine shafts situated at the very edge of the county's rugged coastline.

The world of Cornwall's hardrock mines has its own lore and a complex social history rooted in Cornish national identity. 'If there is a hole anywhere on earth,' goes a traditional saying, 'you're sure to find a Cornishman at the bottom of it.' The conditions in the mines were, not surprisingly, terrible. The air was thick with soot and other poisonous substances, like arsenic, and the shafts, unlike coal mines, weren't ventilated, meaning there was buildup of so-called 'vitiated air' – i.e., carbon dioxide exhaled by other miners.

During the mid-nineteenth century, when Britain's Industrial Revolution was at its peak, the mines were worked not just by men but also children – an 1842 Royal Commission documented the horrendous conditions. But, as a 1999 essay in the *Journal of the Royal Society of Medicine* pointed out, change came slowly:

> The descent to the rock face was by means of almost vertical ladders and took the miners up to an hour before reaching the bottom of the shaft. Likewise, after an eight-hour shift, they had a two-hour climb to reach grass, and it was a matter of honour amongst the younger men not to stop for breath during the entire climb. Much was made during early investigations of the strain placed on the miners' lungs by such physical exertion, but when mechanical lifts replaced the wooden ladders, the mortality remained high.

How do Cornish pasties fit into this picture? 'Housewives used to make one for each member of the household and mark their initials on one end of the pasty,' the *Guardian* explained. 'The miners carried their pasties to work in a tin bucket which they heated by burning a candle underneath. They threw away the oggies' thick, wide pastry edges after eating the rest of their meal, to avoid being poisoned by tin or copper dust from their fingers.'

A curious footnote: while the Cornish mining industry collapsed by the end of the nineteenth century – the remnants of some of those desolate mines overlooking the Atlantic are now protected as World Heritage Sites – there's a small but active Cornish pasty sector in Mexico, of all places, a gastronomical legacy of the migration of Cornish miners.

The years following the Cornish pasty's coronation as a heritage food has been a period of, well, culinary innovation, not all of it welcome. 'Great British Bake-Off Champ Nadiya Hussain "Peas-Off" Cornish Pasty Purists,' shouted a 2017 headline on a story about the controversial decision to add peas – a move that, the paper claimed, 'sparked outrage' across Cornwall. The next year, however, an American chef from Virginia, Mike Burgess, won the World Pasty Championship with a recipe that involved a filling made from pineapples, pulled chicken, yams, and barbecue sauce. Apparently, it was the first time an American had beaten the Cornish at their own game. As Burgess said, 'We have always been focused on fusion.' The CPA welcomed the result, though possibly with a stiff upper lip.

The incidental question lurking in the wings of the convoluted story of the Cornish pasty's origins has to do with whether pasties are an English form of dumpling. They're certainly included in published surveys of dumplings (e.g., *A World of Dumplings*, by cookbook author Brian Yarvin), as well as works by online amateurs, like DumplingHunter.net, a blog dedicated to dumpling sightings. 'If we begin with the definition that a dumpling is a sealed pocket of dough that encloses a savory or sweet filling, then I think the Pasty counts as the English dumpling,' DumplingHunter opined in a 2012 post. 'Pasties are baked and a lot larger than your typical Asian dumpling, but,' as DH adds, 'an uncooked Pasty looks a lot like a Chinese dumpling.'

Some Cornish pasty enthusiasts, needless to say, have turned that equation around. CornishPasties.org.uk, a website brimming with pasty trivia past and present, points out that pasties have been found in faraway locales like Japan. They're also known as gyozas.

The Round Ambassador

Jennifer Jordan

In September 2005, the agricultural minister of Upper Austria, a province bordering Bavaria, called a press conference to announce a campaign bringing attention to the dumplings of Upper Austria as a tourist attraction and an alternative to pizza and hamburgers. He noted the appointment of a 'Dumpling Manager' to oversee an effort to increase the visibility and availability of dumplings. Dumplings, he said, would place Upper Austria on the culinary map, enticing visitors to the region and drawing them into restaurants across the province. But how could lumps of boiled dough warrant their own press conference, not to mention the sense that they somehow conveyed enough of a regional identity to act as a 'round ambassador' for the province?

The Austrian dumpling exemplifies some of the ways that relatively cheap ingredients become both strikingly symbolic and profoundly filling. There are three primary lessons to be learned from these Austrian dumplings that suddenly found themselves in the limelight and warranting press conferences.

First, a dumpling, like many other foods, is ripe for both powerful symbolism and changing meanings. The meanings invested in dumplings, as with other foods, may vary from the very private level of a kind of Proustian remembrance from childhood, to dumplings as symbols of regions or nations, as objects of fading nostalgia, or active entrepreneurial campaigns to boost the economies and external identities of particular regions. Like many foods, including the beloved, labour-intensive Vietnamese New Year rice cakes described by Nir Avieli, the dumplingesque banh tet, dumplings are polyvalent, capable of invoking or bearing multiple and even contradictory meanings. Dumplings, like other foods, can become the screens on which people project meanings, as well as the vehicles for the consumption of particular messages.

A second lesson is that the dumpling is an example of a homemade and relatively inexpensive food that nonetheless has broad cross-class appeal. While dumplings can have something luxurious about them, as with rolling carts full of steaming dim sum and great platters of empanadas, they also are clearly often a response to tough times – a way to stretch a bit of filling into a satisfying meal.

Third, the dumpling contains a complex geopolitical history, a story of simultaneous rootedness and mobility. The tale encompasses the raw materials of food (such as potatoes or wheat), of people, of the shifting borders of, in this case, the Austro-Hungarian Empire, and the movement of people across the surface of the earth. People, food, recipes, appetites, habits, cooking pots, cookbooks, even monastery gardens circulate and spread the word about culinary and horticultural trends, as do travellers and immigrants. Various dumpling histories cite the centrality of Bohemia as a dumpling homeland, from which Central European dumpling culture radiated outward. Further, the dumpling promotion campaign mentioned above is part of a much larger movement in Europe – and much of the rest of the world – that uses food to brand particular places and uses particular places to brand particular foods.

A DUMPLING LEXICON

The English language is ill-suited to handle the German words for dumplings. Nockerln, Spätzle, Knödel, Kloss, Klösschen, Buchteln, Krapfen (which are sometimes like fritters or crullers but at other times more closely resemble ravioli), Taschen, and Tascherln are just the beginning. Many dumplings are named for their place of origin, but even in these cases the actual recipes may vary by family, village, valley, or region. The words also reflect language differences (German, Austrian, Bohemian, Bavarian), and to the well-trained ear and palate may imply differences of shape or substance.

In addition to (and in part actually causing) this linguistic diversity and confusion is the sheer heterogeneity of dumplings themselves – even if one only examines those today classified as Austrian or Central European (not to mention the astonishing global dumpling diversity). In the introduction to a tiny dumpling cookbook focused on the German-speaking world, Oda Tietz writes:

> from rustic to elegant, from big (like a tennis ball) to delicate and small (like a cherry), presented in bowls, on plates or platters … Whether prepared from raw or boiled potatoes, from flour or semolina, day-old rolls, meat, quark [somewhere between cottage cheese, sour cream, and cream cheese; referred to as Topfen in Austria], or yeast, furnished with fine fillings, packed into napkins as so-called 'large' dumplings or as a 'cozy' accompaniment to delicious, crispy, and hearty roasts – they are irresistible …

In her overview of dumplings, she includes not only the savoury varieties, but also sweet ones: 'Cherries, apricots, apples, pears, plums, blueberries, strawberries, poppy seeds or buttermilk … Marillen dumplings, cream cheese dumplings, milk dumplings …'

So, while much about dumplings defies precise categorization or definition, it is at least possible to distinguish between sweet and savoury dumplings. Savoury may be served in a soup, as a side dish, or, as in the case of Bratknödel, as a main course.

Sweet dumplings are by no means limited to dessert and belong to the broad category of flour-based foods that can be meals unto themselves, often called Mehlspeisen. Blind dumplings are those without filling. Liver dumplings (Leberknödel) are a way of serving a piece of liver that may not be good on its own – a bit of beef liver (preferably ground by a butcher, according to one cookbook) mixed with stale bread crumbs, onion, parsley, a little butter, an egg, and some spices. These dumplings, served floating in a rich broth, are extremely filling.

There are debates regarding the geographic origins of savoury dumplings. H. Etzlstorfer writes: 'The classic Dumpling province is Tyrol with its great variety of bacon, spinach, or cheese (Kaspressknödeln), that are used as a side dish and eaten in soup.'

In Upper Austria, the proximity to Bohemia and Bavaria shapes the menu, which contains many dumpling dishes. The culinary skills of a cook are often measured by her ability to prepare dumplings. Indeed, when making Bratknödeln in an Upper Austrian village many years ago, I was warned that any hint of fat floating on the surface of the water (having escaped from a poorly sealed dumpling) would cast doubt on my marriageability.

Dumplings may have bits of meat in them that many people would be unlikely to eat on their own. Bratknödelbrat is not simply a meatball by another name and would be unappetizing without the alchemy of dough and boiling water, and served with another inexpensive but nourishing food, like cabbage. Grammelknödel are a potato dough surrounding fried cracklings that create a sticky, sweet gravy inside the protective layer of potato and are reminiscent of Chinese steamed pork buns.

Some dumpling cookbooks contain recipes for bone marrow dumplings (marrow mixed with bread crumbs, an egg, and milk, then quickly boiled). Some recipes are simply for pockets of dough stuffed with brain, or bread dumplings stuffed with sausage. There are Carinthian Cheese Noodles (Kärntner Kasnudeln), which qualify as dumplings, although they come close to being very hefty ravioli. One cookbook opens the Kasnudeln recipes with an anecdote about the importance of a woman's ability to make them to attract a man.

Kartoffelknödel (the German version) or Erdäpfelknödel (the Austrian version) can be made with a powdered mix in a box, or with a couple of boiled floury potatoes, milled and mixed with eggs, flour, and semolina. Potato dumplings can be stuffed with ground beef, veal, pork, cracklings, or apricots. Spinach dumplings turn into massive dark green balls, stuffed and topped with white cheese. Dumplings can also (albeit more rarely) be filled with lamb, pork, goose, chanterelles, venison liver, venison, and chestnuts. A key difference between Knödel and Taschen or Tascherl seems to be shape. Knödel are round (and generally have a thicker dough flattened by hand), whereas pockets (or Tascherl) are often half-moon-shaped, with a thinner, rolled dough.

Dumplings are also a way of extending food without the use of preservatives. With Semmelknödel, there is a progression from the stale, rock-hard kaiser rolls that home cooks keep in their pantries (waiting until there are enough to make a batch of dumplings), to the dumplings themselves, served freshly made alongside a slice of some kind of roasted meat, to the dish served with leftover dumplings, Geröstete Knödel. Here Semmelknödel are cut into thick slices revealing the layers of bread crumbs, fried in some oil and butter with soft onions, and served with scrambled eggs and parsley. This cheap, filling dish is available in restaurants and taverns throughout Vienna and is generally listed as vegetarian.

Some Semmelknödel recipes call for a bit of pork fat, but they are often made with no meat (although an egg or two is used to bind the mass together). Nockerl and Spätzle are another category frequently available in down-to-earth restaurants. Spätzle are tiny dumplings, not stuffed with anything but put through a Spätzle sieve or slid off a cutting board with the back of a knife, then dropped into boiling water, and often served with bits of bacon, eggs, and/or cheese. Griessnockerl are made of semolina flour, eggs, and butter, and often appear in bowls of broth.

Many unfilled dumplings in Central Europe are meant to serve as an accompaniment to meat, and each dumpling has its appropriate match. I once made the mistake of serving potato dumplings with a caraway pork roast and braised red cabbage instead of with goose, which is a more traditional accompaniment to that combination of dumpling and cabbage – my guests made it clear that this was incorrect, despite being delicious. There are also recent trends toward more herb- or vegetable-infused dumplings. My Upper Austrian cookbook includes Bärlauchnockerln, small dumplings like gnocchi made from ramson, or wild garlic (available only for a brief period in the spring, before it gets too old and slightly poisonous), and then mixed with the usual combination of eggs, Topfen, potatoes, flour, and bread crumbs.

A favourite Austrian fruit dumpling is the Marillenknödel, which uses apricots – preferably those from the Wachau Valley. The cook pops the pit out of a ripe apricot with a finger or the handle of a wooden spoon, fills the void with a sugar cube or lump of marzipan, then wraps the apricot in a layer of floury potato dough. The dumpling is boiled and served in browned bread crumbs and butter, with a sprinkling of sugar. Sometimes they serve as a midday meal, particularly on warm summer days.

There are many varieties of the Salzburger Nockerl, a massive dessert that looks very little like a dumpling, despite its name. In one of their cookbooks, star Austrian cook Ewald Plachutta and cookbook author Christoph Wagner warn that 'the success of the Salzburger dumpling [which can be as big as a lasagna] demands precision, a greaseless cold "Schnee-kessel" [a bowl for whipping egg whites, referred to as Schnee, or snow], as well as quick action.' There are also capuchin dumplings, yeast dumplings, and tiny snow dumplings made from whipped egg whites dropped in boiling water.

BETWEEN POVERTY AND PLENTY

Dumplings speak simultaneously of poverty and plenty. They are a way of turning stale bread or hunks of pork fat into a filling, flavourful meal and can be physically and even emotionally nourishing. Dumplings in Central Europe are typically made by women at home and require a fair amount of work, so sitting down to a plate full of dumplings often implies female labour in the background.

In the Czech Republic, dumplings are an important element of national and culinary identity. 'Meat and dumpling based dishes are not only associated with the traditional and Czech, they are also associated with a certain kind of masculinity involving notions of male strength,' Norwegian anthropologist Haldes Haukanes wrote in 2003. Women, who at the time tended to do the cooking in the Bohemian countryside, said that men expect meat and dumplings as often as possible. Yet younger and urban women interviewed in 2003 often did not know how to make the dumplings and resorted (sometimes with embarrassment) to ready-made dumplings. Thus the meaning and consumption of dumplings has been in transition alongside changes in gender roles and workday schedules.

One cookbook put together as a benefit for a Viennese homeless shelter was filled with recipes that could be made by shelter residents (i.e., meals costing less than five euros), including a recipe for potato dumplings stuffed with bits of blood sausage and another for bacon dumplings made of day-old rolls and a little bacon.

But in other eras and other places, dumplings were not regarded as fare for the poor. In *On Food and Cooking*, Harold McGee points out that Chinese dumplings have at various times been considered a sign of wealth and good taste, rather than the food of the poor. 'Around 300 CE, Shu Xi wrote an ode to wheat products (bing) that names several kinds of noodles and dumplings, describes how they're made, and suggests their luxurious qualities,' he writes. 'Noodles – *mian* or *mein* – and filled dumplings began in the north as luxury foods for the ruling class. They gradually became staples of the working class, with dumplings retaining the suggestion of prosperity … '

Thus, dumplings have bounced (figuratively) around the scale of socio-economic status and vary on the plate from side to centre, and on the menu from soup to dessert. They often express home cooking rather than haute cuisine, especially in Bavaria, Austria, and the Czech Republic, but there are efforts to elevate dumplings (and many other home-made countryside products) to the point where they are served not only in backyards and family kitchens, but also in fine restaurants and in fashionable resort areas.

THE 'ROUND AMBASSADOR'

A 2006 article titled 'A Round Ambassador for Upper Austria' asserts that 'Upper Austria is the kingdom of dumplings.' Yet, no matter how they are arranged on a plate, dumplings simply do not look like more conventional haute cuisine. They may be served (and photographed) whole as glistening orbs, or sliced down the middle to reveal the stuffing, or artfully arranged as perfectly styled delicate slices of bread dumplings, draped with strips of omelette and a dusting of herbs. As an Upper Austrian cookbook by Ingrid Pemkopf and Christoph Wagner concludes, 'the dumpling lends itself perfectly to being a culinary trademark.'

The publicity campaign about the humble dumpling was a way to bolster gastronomy and tourism, drawing visitors to the region in search of culinary pleasures. It sought to elevate the rank of the dumpling, to pull it out of the kitchen and onto the dinner tables of tourists or into the kitchens of professional chefs, but also to market it as a very bodenständig (down-to-earth) cuisine.

Cookbooks aligned with the campaign presented stories on the dumpling's archaeological origins and regional credit-taking. 'Culinary archaeology dates its first "Dumpling" find (at the very least a "dough find") to the Neolithic piling dwelling villages established along the Mondsee (a lake in Upper Austria) between 2500 and 1800 BC,' wrote Plachutta and Wagner. 'The primary realm of the dumpling is Upper Austria and Bavaria, as well as southern Bohemia, Tyrol, and South Tyrol, which also belong, in culinary terms, to the territory of the dumpling.'

Upper Austria's promotional dumpling materials reached the public in print form, on television and radio, on the inter net, in cookbooks, and at public events. 'A Longing for Regionalism in a Globalizing World,' read the headline of one of the press releases, which also mentioned dumpling stalls and cooking demonstrations at local farmers' markets. The campaign also stressed how dumplings embodied, to some extent, national or regional identity, but there was often something tongue-in-cheek about this project. As much as dumplings are adored, they are treated with less gravity than foie gras or Parmigiano Reggiano.

There is as yet no protected status for dumplings, as there is for so many other European foods, everything from Cognac to Champagne, Portuguese honey to Polish cheese, but culinary place-marketing is definitely a strategy many regional governments and chambers of commerce or agricultural boards are embracing. Fundamental to this work is crafting or coalescing narratives that make food recognizable and unique, as Upper Austria's dumpling campaign demonstrated. In Upper Austria and elsewhere, they reveal the connections between the cultural and the culinary, the local and the global, and the many ways in which the simplest foods can also be powerfully complex.

Red Wine and Empanadas

John Lorinc

In early September 1970, Salvador Allende led a socialist coalition, the Unidad Popular, to victory in a national Chilean election that caught much of the West off guard. A veteran of Chile's left, Allende swept to power on the strength of a platform that, he vowed, would promote a homegrown program of reform rather than reheated Soviet-style communism.

To demonstrate his commitment, he famously pledged to lead a revolution 'flavoured with red wine and empanadas' – something, in other words, that would be uniquely Chilean.

Though empanadas are standard fare in much of Latin America, the Chilean versions tend to be larger and rectangular. 'The Chilean empanada habit came from Spain, where empanadas have been documented since the 13th century,' noted *New York Times* food writer Florence Fabricant in 2009. 'To Chileans, empanadas mostly mean *empanadas al horno*, which are frequently baked in a wood-burning oven. The classic versions are filled with seasoned minced (not ground) meat and onions and garnished with hard-cooked egg, olives and raisins. They can be made either in the half-moon shape … or in a distinctively Chilean squared-off form made by folding all but the straight side of the semicircular turnover to make a package that is often four inches across.'

Allende's romantic vision of Chilean socialism lasted for just three years, until he was deposed during a junta led by the CIA-backed general Augusto Pinochet, who imposed a brutal dictatorship that endured for sixteen years. (Allende killed himself.)

There's no question that certain foods have become strongly identified with specific national identities – Scottish haggis, American hamburgers, Italian pasta, Japanese sushi. Yet the story of Allende's election slogan shows how some dishes can also flip over into the realm of the political – as strongly imbued with meaning as with seasoning.

The Roman poet Juvenal coined the expression 'bread not circuses' in response to the political tactic of governments deploying extravagant displays or events as a way to distract public attention from pressing issues. In Toronto in the late 1980s, anti-poverty activists resurrected the phrase when they formed the Bread Not Circuses Coalition to oppose the city's bid for the 1996 Olympics at a time of housing shortages and rising homelessness.

During Hungary's postwar Stalinist era, the country's leader, Mátyás Rákosi, is said to have invented the gastronomically evocative phrase 'salami tactics' to describe the process of slicing away at his political opponents' power bit by bit – a technique that the country's current illiberal president, Viktor Orbán, has resurrected, in practice if not in name, to strip power from independent media and opposition parities one edict at a time. (In 1981, a *Washington Post* columnist observed that Poland's 'liberalizing' communist government, under pressure from the Solidarity movement, was engaged in 'reverse salami tactics' – i.e., adding new freedoms bit by bit, much like Mikhail Gorbachev did in the final years of the Soviet Union.)

Generations before Salvador Allende transformed the Chilean empanada into a potent symbol of nationalist defiance, dumpling politics had surfaced in Latin America's long struggle with its colonial roots. In the early twentieth century, some Mexican modernizers argued strenuously for an end to the use of maize in the production of tamales, a stuffed dumpling that was a traditional staple among Indigenous communities. Maize, the reformers claimed, was an inferior ingredient to wheat, lacking in protein. 'In 1901,' writes food historian Rachel Laudan in *Cuisine and Empire: Cooking in World History*, 'the criminologist and sociologist Juan Guerrero described tamales (stuffed maize dumplings) as "an abominable outcome of the Mexican popular cooking tradition" and urged Mexicans to adopt French or Spanish cuisine instead.'

More recently, dumplings have been deployed as perhaps unexpected props in political conflicts. In 2021, for example, hundreds of Indian Youth Congress delegates staged a protest in Mumbai against rapidly rising oil prices by feeding gulab jamun – a sweet dessert dumpling served in rose-water-infused syrup – to donkeys. The gesture was meant to underscore the impact of the rising fuel prices on edible oils, a key ingredient.

Other dumpling deployments have been far less theatrical. As Julie Van Rosendaal points out in 'The Perogy Bees of the Prairies' (page 162), the Russian invasion of Ukraine, which began in late February 2022, spurred hundreds of pierogi-themed fundraisers, as Ukrainian expat communities sold thousands of dumplings to raise funds for the defence of the country.

Distant wars or conflicts, meanwhile, have spilled into the consumerist world of North American dining. In 2017, the *Washington Post* reported on the much-anticipated opening of D.C.'s first Uyghur restaurants, eateries whose very existence (a form of 'culinary diplomacy,' as the paper noted) served to remind U.S. diners about China's campaign of suppression and cultural genocide against the Muslim minority located in the country's northwest province.

The owners offered a range of Uyghur dishes, including distinctive noodles, known as lagman, that are 'hand-pulled, dense and always a little chewy.' As the *Post*'s reviewer explained, 'the same dough goes into manta, beef or pumpkin-stuffed dumplings that are traditionally served for very special guests. The length of the noodles may perplex some American diners: The goal is to have "Just one noodle."'

'Uyghur food is going to be the next big thing in the United States,' Yimamu Maimaiti, a partner in the first Uyghur restaurant to open in the region, predicted. 'Uyghur food is going to be in every corner in the world.'

Given that the Uyghurs come from the same region of Asia that produced the thirteenth-century Mongol ruler

Genghis Khan, whose vast empire produced a continental trail of dumpling variants (sanbusak, samosa, manti, vareniki, and even ravioli), Maimaiti's ambitions may foreshadow the world's next great culinary exodus.

Dumplingware:
The Allure of Porcelain

Marie Campbell

It's what we do, my younger daughter and I. She flies home and, before even exiting the airport parking lot, we've called in our dumpling soup order. So much changes in her young life between visits – *she* changes; I do, too, a bit – that a stop at 'our' dumpling house is a comforting reminder of common tastes and shared years. Yet, as deliciously distracting as the dumpling soup or my daughter's latest news is, I will always spare a bit of attention for how we eat and serve the foods we love. This particular soup, I know, comes in blue-and-white bowls and is eaten with a flat-bottomed spoon perfectly designed to deliver both broth and dumpling in a single slurp. May this stubbornly unrenovated dumpling house never switch up any of it!

Many of the most ubiquitous examples of material culture are food-related, of course. Dumplings themselves might be the platinum-tier travellers of global comfort food, but a preference for one type over another isn't the only taste we humans carry as we move around the globe. We also pack stuff, the *things* we love. The cast-iron pot that cooks goulash, ginger-flavoured soup, or a whole chicken. The platter used every week for generations to serve up the Sunday roast.

If food history reveals how people's paths have crossed and foodstuffs cross-pollinated, the actual dishes we use tell stories, too. Theirs are fascinating examples of the intersection of different kinds of human hungers, and none is more interesting than the history of porcelain.

The bowls at my modest dumpling house are actually plastic. But the reference is obvious: to china, immediately recognizable with its familiar decoration. But why 'china' or, sometimes, 'chinaware'? Because for thousands of years, only the Chinese knew how to make porcelain, a uniquely beautiful form of vitrified pottery that's also non-porous, and thus ideally suited to holding food of all kinds.

First perfected during the Tang dynasty (618–907 CE), the smooth porcelain we recognize today is tricky to make. The precise recipe and temperatures at which to fire the clay mixture into translucency – let alone how, exactly, to build kiln heat to the requisite 1305°C to 1346°C range – was for centuries one of China's most jealously guarded state secrets. And wisely so: consumers loved porcelain and were prepared to pay dearly for it. It became one of the world's first transnational products, an early global commodity.

Initially traded by China to the Islamic world in exchange for the cobalt-blue dye that creates the distinctive blue underglaze, luminous porcelain goods made their way along the Silk Road and ultimately to Europe by the sixteenth century. There, they quickly became objects of intense elite desire, instant signifiers of the owner's status and wealth. By the late seventeenth century, all of Europe's nobility and every other brand of social climber was collectively felled by what became known as 'porcelain sickness' (more evocatively, Porzellankrankheit). A staggering statistic: by the close of the eighteenth century, at least seventy million pieces of porcelain had been imported to Europe alone.

Not all those pieces ended up in the collection of the memorably named Saxon noble Augustus the Strong, but that wasn't for lack of trying. Compulsively attracted to extravagance and competitive consumerism, Augustus, once the King of Poland, ultimately possessed in the range of 35,000 pieces of porcelain. 'It is the same with porcelain as with oranges,' the manic collector once confessed in a letter. 'If you have a longing for the one or the other, you will never have enough.'

The Elector of Saxony and, for a time, Grand Duke of Lithuania, Augustus left a legacy of many bottomless appetites when he died in 1733. For women: he's estimated to have fathered at least 365 illegitimate children. For power: he bribed and warred his way to those many titles. For wine and food: even in an immoderate era, Augustus's days-long bacchanals were infamous. Were there dumplings on his laden luncheon table? Maybe. Probably. Likely, even: fellow contributor Jennifer Jordan tells us elsewhere in this collection that dumplings are to Augustus's part of the world what pizza is to Italy or chocolate to Switzerland.

But that's not really why the hand of Augustus still helps serve our dumpling soup today. Rather, it's because his voracious appetite for porcelain landed him seriously in debt. And debt makes people do desperate things. En route to amassing his unrivalled collection, Augustus depleted his royal treasuries. So much money for porcelain purchases flowed back to China – described wryly by one of his court officials as 'the bleeding bowl of Saxony' – that Augustus turned to magic to solve his problems, magic in this case masquerading as the 'science' of alchemy.

What happens next in this story is better than Hollywood. If some enterprising director hasn't yet snapped up screen rights to journalist Janet Gleeson's stylish and pacey *The Arcanum: The Extraordinary True Story of the Invention of European Porcelain*, that's a boat being missed. In his search for funds, Augustus falls for the claims of an alchemist-swindler named Johann Friedrich Bottger to know the formula for turning lead into gold. Thinking he's found the solution to his problems, Augustus kidnaps Bottger, locking him in a basement laboratory-cum-prison with the proviso that his freedom can be won only by producing gold. Unfortunately for both Augustus and his alchemist, the gold refused to be made. After several dramatic escape attempts, the miserable Bottger, sickened by the metals and chemicals with which he worked, didn't catch a break until the frustrated Augustus sent in an older, wiser scientist to rescue the operation.

What Ehrenfried Walther von Tschirnhaus, a German scientist, suggested to Bottger was as much a shift in marketing as it was in chemistry. He proposed that the duo search instead for *white* gold, which is to say, for the technique of producing porcelain. In 1708, after their experiments had destroyed countless kilns, buildings, and lives, they cracked the recipe. With Augustus as financial backer, the Meissen porcelain factory was established in 1710–15 to feed Europe's insatiable demand. That factory still operates today in Meissen, Germany, and its signature blue crossed-swords logo is among the oldest trademarks in existence.

Like the generations of Chinese porcelain producers and merchants before them, the managers at the Meissen factory originally tried desperately to keep the porcelain arcanum to and for themselves. They effectively imprisoned workers within factory confines and limited the number of staff 'in the know.' Punishment for leaks was death. But the secret got out, of course. Rivals funded in-factory spies to steal the technology and then set up competing factories, increasing production and depressing prices. As the emerging European (then English, then North American) middle classes were able to afford porcelain and its imitators, its ubiquity exploded. Once a signifier of wealth for only the very rich, porcelain became – and still is – a show of more modest affluence for a now-broad swath of the consumer market.

Shards of former porcelain plates, vases, keepsakes of all kinds, are excavated from archaeological digs the world over. Some intact examples might well collect dust in your grand-mother's display hutch. There are likely porcelain pieces in your own cupboards, awaiting dinner. I'd suggest a bowl of dumpling soup. You'll hold in your hands a piece of food history and material culture as adventurous and well-travelled as the dumplings it was designed to contain.

The One True Dumpling

Navneet Alang

Consider it a uniquely modern problem (or perhaps a symptom of something deeply wrong with me personally), but I still recall disagreements I've had on social media from years previous. Among the litany of slights and debates in my mind, one came from a well-intentioned student, complaining about experimental samosa flavours she had found: some little fried pastry pockets at a local store filled with – the horror! – cream cheese and raspberry jam.

The outrage, of course, was that these were a bastardization of the samosa, and yet another example of how non-Western foods are both appropriated and corrupted in an effort to appeal to Western tastes.

What made this quite ordinary complaint memorable – and also quite wrong – was that, first, the establishment in question was run and owned by Indo-Canadians; and second, that the samosa, far from being a uniquely or purely Indian concoction, is also found among cultures in the Middle East, East Africa, and Central Asia – and, thanks to their various and massive diasporas, all across the world.

Put more plainly: there is no one, true samosa from which to deviate. And even if there were, wouldn't the very cultures crafting them have free rein to make them as they saw fit?

This paradox is the difficult thing about assertions of authenticity or ownership when it comes to food. While we cannot simply dismiss the long legacy of cultural appropriation and the dismissal of so-called 'foreign' food, whose definition of authenticity actually constitutes the true one?

But then, the samosa, as the Central Asian manifestation of the dumpling, was always bound to be wrapped up in contests of what is and is not true. Given the millennia-long history of empires, colonization, and intermingling in the region, mixture was inevitable. Just as my parents' first language of Punjabi melds Sanskrit-derived words with Persian and Arabic ones – as befits its speakers' position precisely between the Middle East and the subcontinent – so, too, does the Indian samosa blend the Middle Eastern and broadly South Asian into a new mixture.

Yet dumplings and dumpling-like foods are particularly ripe for both experimentation and the related questions that emerge. As with the sandwich, the ubiquity, comparative ease, and even portability of dumplings lend themselves to the sort of mix and match approach to food that can make cooking fun and cuisine interesting – throw this filling into that wrapper and let's see what happens.

Find yourself at either a dumpling stall or fancy restaurant in many places across the world, and the open canvas of the dumpling will reveal itself. Sometimes mixtures are more like cousins: butter chicken momos meld Tibetan and Indian, while bulgogi gyoza might combine Korean and Japanese. At other times, they are more global in nature, as with Jamaican patties filled with Filipino adobo, or Chinese wontons packed with Spanish chorizo.

As delicious as those combinations are, they do present something of a puzzle. On the one hand, the fusion of differing cultural elements is how novelty and innovation occur. Tinkering with flavours and ingredients is how both cuisines and cultures evolve, but it also fuels the market's desire for new things over which to obsess. It's how we get, say, the ubiquity of Nashville hot chicken, pineapple pizza, or even just spaghetti and meatballs.

At its most ideal, fusion cuisine becomes part of a new national identity – one that emerges when a formerly marginalized culture is folded into a newly changed 'mainstream.' It's why the British so eagerly embraced curry and chips or why we in Canada gobble up things like jerk chicken poutine.

And let us not forget another key point: fusion dishes like this are also just tasty.

On the other hand, the fusing of cultural cuisines can sometimes feel quite off or incongruous. Talk to an Italian nonna about pineapple on pizza or hunks of chicken in your weeknight pasta and it would be wise to remain out of reach of her rolling pin. The ideal, hardly unique to the Mediterranean, is that food is made in a certain fashion because it is best that way. It's not just that the individual dish is meant to taste as it does, but that said dish fits into the cuisine of a certain place, such that a plate of spaghetti is eaten in small quantities prior to another course, not on giant plates that would make a nutritionist cry.

Yet when fusion cuisine is devoid of context or done crassly to maximize sales, it can sometimes continue a frustrating legacy. It is only a slight stretch to see the appropriation of Eastern cuisines by Western corporate behemoths as a legacy of colonial exploitation. While, obviously, no one is harmed when a mom-and-pop shop produces a dumpling that mixes Asian and Caribbean flavours, one can't exactly say the same thing when a chain restaurant does it. After all, isn't a mostly white mainstream company profiting off the cuisine of denigrated cultures its own form of exploitation – a way of, yet again, taking from racialized minorities with no recompense?

It's tricky stuff, which is why some people harden their positions into one of two extremes: all fusion is fine or none of it is. Both, however, are unsatisfactory, and not just because of their shaky ideological predication; they're also just boring. Imagine a world in which either no culinary mingling occurred or, worse, where the history of our connection to food had been erased.

Another wrinkle, though, is that the conversation about food and cultural appropriation is tinged with the rose-coloured discourse about food being a gateway to other cultures. That hoary old cliché is, as it turns out, not particularly true. Tens of millions of people can pile noodles and curries onto their plates and still be perfectly racist. The only thing food can do is serve as a quiet reminder that there are other ways of doing and being, and there are many people who are all too happy not to listen.

Yet for all the politics, there is also something pleasing, and even satisfying, about inauthenticity. The great swath of immigrants and migrants all across the world who do not fit easily into neat cultural categories are themselves also inauthentic. They are neither this nor that, but rather some ever-shifting mix of cultures, irreducibly multiple. And food, like music or other forms of culture that are intimately or even bodily connected to pleasure, can always escape its historical antecedents because it is also just a sensation, a feeling: a biochemical and neurological reaction to stimuli that produces happiness or satisfaction. History is important, but even history cannot interrupt the shudder of pleasure that comes from, oh, let's say a thin, starchy wrapper filled with mushrooms, gruyere, and black truffle.

What, then, might we say about the impossible choice between the assertion that the dumpling is either everyone's or belongs to only those who can, by moral authority, claim to own it?

It would, perhaps, be too obvious to argue that the dumpling is a neat little metaphor for the inauthenticity of cultural mixture – a sort of interruption of coherent national narratives about identity and belonging. Too obvious, and also too pat. Something in that comparison both elides the complexity of the politics of the culinary while also placing too much weight on a small morsel of food. We're talking about just a siu mai or a samosa – not the whole kaleidoscopic breadth of human experience.

Maybe think of my question this way: the dumpling, like all food, is simultaneously just sustenance – a mere snack – but also history, culture, creativity, and the terrain upon which mixture and the impossibility of a single narrative of authenticity play out. There is, to be a bit trite, no one true dumpling, but there are multiple, competing narratives about what the one true dumpling actually is – including the idea that it doesn't matter at all.

The question of the dumpling's essence is frustratingly indeterminate, but then the most important things about being human tend to be. There are times when the history of a dumpling recipe matters greatly, and times when it doesn't matter at all – moments when the purity of a cuisine is important and others when it should be roundly and aggressively challenged. You'll have to forgive me when I say, only half ironically: it's Schrödinger's samosa.

The task of the invested cultural critic, though, is not to determine which is the one true dumpling, but if and when a certain story about the one true dumpling should be brought to bear. What fills the dumpling can be important, but it is the narrative around it that counts – and it is only when one masticates and ruminates on both that we get closer to what is actually true.

Conclusion

Culinary Carry-On

John Lorinc

In the midst of Toronto's 2010 municipal election, my mother had a stroke. I had been assigned to cover the campaign of the hapless candidate who ended up being steamrollered by Rob Ford's proto-Trumpian populism. For the most part, all I remember of that fall is bouncing between hospitals and press conferences. Over the months that followed, my mother made a partial recovery while my sister Julie and I put into place the architecture of her new normal – a life that now included a retirement home, physiotherapists, walkers, wheelchairs, etc.

Such events disrupt everything, including, and perhaps especially, family traditions, one of which was an annual fall dinner featuring a Hungarian delicacy called szilvás gombóc – plum dumplings. These are made with a potato dough that envelopes a prune plum that's had the pit swapped out for a sugar cube. They're boiled, then fried in a mixture of bread crumbs and oil, and finally served with more sugar infused with lemon rind.

Very labour-intensive. Very delicious. Very heavy. Consumed as the main, although my wife, Victoria, who questions this tradition's devotion to the Mitteleuropa ideal of dessert-as-entree, has long insisted on adding a salad to provide some semblance of nutritional value.

The first fall after my mother's stroke, it became clear that Julie and I would have to take over the making of the plum dumplings. We asked her for instructions – an epic mistake. My mother rhymed off the ingredients: flour, a large potato, plums, sugar cubes.

'You'll need a potato ricer,' she added.

A *what*?

In the WASPy world of North Toronto in the 1960s and 1970s, my mother's kitchen was, in every way, a place with a mixing spoon in two worlds. Faced with all sorts of social and consumer pressures to assimilate, my mother had a repertoire that included many of the pillars of postwar cuisine: Campbell's soup, KD, mini-pizzas, Wonder bread, etc. She made mains like roast beef and Yorkshire pudding, and Chicken à la King, but also the Hungarian staples she grew up with, like stuffed green peppers and stuffed cabbage, as well as a few sui generis specialties that are inexplicable to the uninitiated: a dish involving egg noodles, cottage cheese, and bacon bits, and a wildly delicious starch-fest called rakott krumpli, which is a third cousin of scalloped potatoes but involves a lot of dried sausage, hard-boiled eggs, and sour cream.

When I reached Grade 7 and began taking lunch to school, my sandwiches were likely to be kifli buns (chewy, crescent-shaped, and encrusted with salt and caraway seeds) filled with slices of the aforementioned dried sausage (csabai). The other kids were packing bologna or PB&J with a side of celery sticks. Kifli and csabai is what passed for exotic at the time.

Dumplings were very much a part of the picture, and not just the plum variety. My mother regularly made túrógombóc, which substitute a Hungarian type of cottage cheese for the plums and can be eaten sweet or savoury. (I preferred these as a kid because I was an absurdly picky eater and didn't like the texture of cooked plum skin.) She also made, once in a while, something I now recognize as a Hungarian version of gnocchi: knuckle-sized potato-dough dumplings, boiled and then breaded (you can see a pattern here). The unpronounceable Hungarian name for this dish is *angyal bogyoro*, which translates roughly – and charmingly! – into English as 'angel's prick.'

Then there was the dessert we had each year on Christmas Eve, which Hungarian Jews (or at least the secular/assimilated type) celebrate with gusto. Most of my parents' friends had such a feast, and the desserts ran to an assortment of Austro-Hungarian pastries. For some reason, the precise origins of which aren't clear, we had something called Gateau St. Honoré, which was most definitely *not* Hungarian. This dessert consists of profiteroles filled with vanilla custard, stacked in a pyramid, covered with a web of caramelized sugar, then served with chocolate custard (it's also known as croquembouche). The shock-and-awe value is off the charts, and this was a dish my mother made precisely once a year.

These were dumplings in drag, extremely tasty and time-consuming. By the time Julie and I were in our teens, we had partly taken over the construction of the Gateau. My mother made the cream puffs a day or two before the twenty-fourth, and then we'd assemble them. My job was to cut each cream puff in two and spoon in a dollop of custard. Julie, in turn, took the top half and applied the hot caramelizing sugar, which could only be made in a copper frying pan used specifically for this purpose. Legend had it that a film of dried sugar remained at the bottom of this pan between uses

– i.e., for 364 days – in order to kick-start the process with each successive production.

I'd say it took Julie and me about a decade to perfect the szilvás gombóc. We replicated the division of labour from the Gateau production line: she made the dough, and I took care of the boiling and frying. This was an expedient for me, I will freely confess. I hate the sensation of dough and flour on my hands and am generally happier in front of a stove than with a rolling pin. The dough, of course, was the hard part. My mother's instructions were, well, imprecise. A 'large potato.' Mix until it 'feels right.' 'Some salt.' That kind of thing.

There was a fair amount of trial and error, with the latter expressing itself further along in the process, once the plum had been encased in dough and plopped into the boiling water. That's the rubber-hits-the-road moment, when you learn if the dough will endure or turn into a sloppy mess. We eventually turned to the internet for help, as one does.

Timing was also an issue, and not just in terms of the cooking. To make szilvás gombóc properly, you need early-fall prune plums, which are intensely seasonal. When they're gone, they're gone. One year, I missed the window and found myself confronted by the problem of finding a replacement.

I asked my younger son, who was working as a chef, for advice. Both my sons used to 'help' their grandmother make plum dumplings when they were little, and there's even a video somewhere in the bowels of YouTube to prove it. He considered the problem carefully and came up with an elegant workaround: we'd buy the larger all-season black plums, cut them in half, take out the pit, excavate some of the insides, then fold the half in half around a sugar cube. His solution worked well and appealed to my own sense of improvisation in the kitchen.

I have always enjoyed cooking – even as a teenager – mainly because I like eating. When I moved away from home, my mother gave me a deck of index cards on which she'd written out some of my favourite foods. Most of these weren't recipes, per se, so much as instructions on how to defrost and reheat these dishes, which she made and deposited at our apartment.

Despite the assist, I built up a repertoire of meals, many sourced from Pierre Franey's *60-Minute Gourmet* books. Here, again, a word about the division of labour: my wife, Victoria, has always worked in an office at the other end of a longish commute, while I worked from home. I became the short-order weekday chef: dinner almost always made from scratch – I genuinely like cutting vegetables while listening to CBC *News* on the grease-encrusted kitchen radio after a day in front of the computer – provided the task can be finished in one hour or less.

On weekends, in turn, Victoria bakes. We are well-suited to our respective tasks. Baking involves precision, attention to detail, a respect for the order of operations – skills she possesses in abundance. I, on the other hand, don't take direction well and have never been especially good at following instructions. I prefer to wing it, and so the recipe is often a kind of starting point – a document to be edited, debated with, and second-guessed.

It's interesting to note in passing how dumplings – not just the ones described above, but elsewhere in this anthology – represent the fusion of both sets of skills. Borrowing from another form of expression, one might say the dough is classical; the filling, jazz.

But there's something else that's fundamental to this amazingly broad genus of foods, and that is the way they pass through both time and space. Many of the stories that make up this anthology begin with recollections of learning a dumpling recipe from a parent or grandparent – all moments that indicate how these foods are intergenerational time travellers. Yet they also move through physical space, accompanying us or our ancestors through immigration, exodus, enslavement, commerce, and conquest, like so much culinary carry-on.

In my research for this essay, I came across an oft-reproduced map, created by food historian Rachel Laudan, showing how dumplings had migrated along trade routes over a period of centuries, from East Asia to India, the Middle East, Central Asia, and finally Eastern Europe. Her map is annotated with names – samosa, manti, kreplach, etc. – and delineated by long, swooping lines that branch off, like the arms of a family tree.

Suffice it to say that dumplings, in all their guises, didn't make these journeys accompanied by anything as definitive as a recipe. The knowledge of how to make them was handed down, parent to child, over countless generations, but not in any fixed sense. This world of dumplings also reveals the inevitable churn of improvisation and change – the incorporation of new ingredients and the evolution of new techniques. Why not fry them? How about leeks instead of turnips, or leaving aside the meat? There are new spices in the market ...

One could argue that dumplings exist in defiance of our era's obsession with lovely cookbooks and five-star online recipes that promise both gastronomical delights *and* authenticity. Perhaps there is such a thing as the perfectly executed matzo ball or samosa – a platonic ideal; indeed, some of the dumplings in this volume speak to the importance of fidelity to culinary traditions. But maybe we can also think of our relationship with the dumplings in our lives in a less custodial way. Switch up the recipe a bit from how you were taught, then pass along your own riff as it proceeds along its temporal journey into the future.

CREDITS

INTRODUCTION

McCurry, Justin. 'Fight to Become Japan's Gyoza Capital Gently Simmers.' *Guardian*, Dec. 23, 2019. https://www.theguardian.com/world/2019/dec/23/fight-to-become-japans-gyoza-capital-gently-simmers-utsunomiya.

Fackler, Marin. 'Insecticide-Tainted Dumplings From China Sicken 175 in Japan.' *New York Times*, Feb. 2, 2008. https://www.nytimes.com/2008/02/02/world/asia/02japan.html.

SINK OR SWIM: A RIFF ON THE ESSENCE OF THE MATZO BALL

I'd like to thank Barbara Kirshenblatt-Gimblett, Michael Wex, and Mark Rubin for background information and resource recommendations. May their matzo balls be always al dente and gently floating.

A SPICY LABOUR OF LOVE

Recipe preparations and variations adapted from The Multi-Cultural Cuisine of Trinidad and Tobago and the Caribbean: Naparima Girls' High School Cookbook, *p. 213, Second Edition, 2002.*

WHAT'S IN A NAME? THE JAMAICAN PATTY CONTROVERSY

Benghait, Norma. *Traditional Jamaican Cookery*. New York: Penguin Books, 1985.

Bradburn, Jamie. 'Historicist: The Toronto Patty Wars,' *Torontoist*, Feb. 5, 2011. www.torontoist.com/2011/02/historicist_the_toronto_patty_wars.

Sainsbury, Brendan. 'How Did a Meal That Combines a Preserved North Atlantic Fish and a Potentially Deadly West African Fruit Become Jamaica's National Dish?' BBC, March 15, 2021. www.bbc.com/travel/article/20210315-ackee-and-saltfish-jamaicas-breakfast-of-champions.

Washington, Bryan. 'The Beef Patty Is Jamaica in the Palm of Your Hand,' *New York Times Magazine*, Feb. 23, 2022. www.nytimes.com/2022/02/23/magazine/beef-patty-recipe.html.

THE ROUND AMBASSADOR

Adapted and shortened with permission from 'Elevating the Lowly Dumpling: From Peasant Kitchens to Press Conferences,' by Jennifer Jordan: Ethnology, Vol. 47, No. 2/3, Spring/Summer 2008.

Avieli, Nir. 'Vietnamese New Year Rice Cakes: Iconic Festive Dishes and Contested National Identity,' *Ethnology* 44(2), 2005.

Etzlstorfer, H., ed. *Küchenkunst und Tafelkultur: Kulinarische Zeugnisse aus der Österreichischen Nationalbibliothek.* Christian Brandstätter Verlag, 2006.

Haukanes, Haldis. 'Ambivalent Traditions: Transforming Gender Symbols and Food Practices in the Czech Republic,' *Anthropology of East Europe Review* 21(1), 2003.

McGee, Harold. *On Food and Cooking: The Science and Lore of the Kitchen.* New York: Scribner, 2004.

Pernkopf, Ingrid, and Christoph Wagner. *Die Oberösterreichische Küche: 520 Klassische Rezepte.* Edition Oberösterreich, 2007.

Plachutta, Ewald, and Christoph Wagner. *Die Gute Küche: Das Österreichische Jahrhundert Kochbuch.* Ora, 1993.

Tietz, Oda. *Das Kleine Knödel Kochbuch.* Hölker Verlag, 2003.

CONTRIBUTORS

Navneet Alang is a Toronto-based cultural critic. His work has appeared in the *Atlantic, Globe and Mail, New York Magazine, Eater, Toronto Star,* and more. He holds a PhD from York University that was technically in English literature but was really just about Twitter.

André Alexis was born in Trinidad and grew up in Canada. His novel *Fifteen Dogs* won the 2015 Scotiabank Giller Prize and the Rogers Writers' Trust Fiction Prize. His debut novel, *Childhood,* won the Books in Canada First Novel Award and the Trillium Book Award, and was shortlisted for the Giller Prize and the Rogers Writers' Trust Fiction Prize. His recent books include *Pastoral, The Hidden Keys, Days by Moonlight* (winner of the Rogers Writers' Trust Fiction Prize), and *Ring.*

Kristen Arnett is the queer author of *With Teeth: A Novel* (Riverhead Books, 2021), which was a finalist for the Lambda Literary Award, and the *New York Times* bestselling debut novel *Mostly Dead Things* (Tin House, 2019), which was also a finalist for the Lambda Literary Award and shortlisted for the VCU Cabell First Novelist Award.

Chantal Braganza is an award-winning writer and deputy editor at *Chatelaine.* Her book, *Guardian Flesh,* is forthcoming from Strange Light.

David Buchbinder is a Grammy-nominated, JUNO Award–winning trumpeter, composer, producer, and cultural inventor. He tours internationally; composes for concert, theatre, film, and television; presents large-scale performance projects; and develops and presents unique community-based creative festivals, performances, and events. His recordings and compositions have enjoyed worldwide release and received international acclaim. David is 'deeply tickled' to now be a published author.

Marie Campbell, an editor and former literary agent, enjoys volunteering at Toronto's Gardiner Museum.

Arlene Chan is a librarian, athlete, artist, author, and historian. She has written several books about Canada's Chinese community, including *Righting Canada's Wrongs: The Chinese Head Tax and Anti-Chinese Immigration Policies in the Twentieth Century*, and has contributed essays to two previous Coach House anthologies, *The Ward* and *The Ward Uncovered*.

Mekhala Chaubal is a Canadian lawyer and writer with roots in India. After growing up across the Middle East, she studied creative writing at Randolph-Macon Woman's College (now Randolph College) in Virginia. Mekhala currently lives in Hamilton with her wife, multiple cats, and houseplants, daydreaming about ways to combine all her lives into stories.

Tatum Taylor Chaubal is a writer and heritage planner. She holds an honours degree in creative writing from Randolph-Macon Woman's College (now Randolph College) and a master's degree in historic preservation from Columbia University. Originally from Texas, she now lives in Ontario with her wife and cats. She has co-edited three anthologies for Coach House Books on the histories and memories of marginalized communities in Toronto.

Naomi Duguid is a writer, photographer, traveller, and home cook who lives in downtown Toronto. Her most recent books are *The Miracle of Salt* (2022), *Taste of Persia*, and *Burma: Rivers of Flavor*.

Eric Geringas immigrated to Canada as a child from Soviet-occupied Latvia, where he developed his love of starchy foods. Since then, he's broadened his palate considerably but still has a passion for potatoes. He is an award-winning writer, documentary filmmaker and TV director, and owner of Power of Babel, a translation company that specializes in subtitling and dubbing.

Christina Gonzales was previously the opinions editor at *Maclean's*. She has won a National Magazine Award for the 'Nanny Diaries,' a *Toronto Life* feature on the lives of Filipino child caregivers. As a content marketer, she has worked with brands like Mejuri, Sephora, Glenfiddich, and Air Canada. She is currently working on her first fiction book.

Jennifer Jordan is a professor of sociology and urban studies at the University of Wisconsin, Milwaukee. She is the author of *Edible Memory: The Lure of Heirloom Tomatoes and other Forgotten Foods* (Chicago, 2015), *Structures of Memory: Understanding Urban Change in Berlin and Beyond* (Stanford, 2006), and *Before Craft Beer: Lost Landscapes of Forgotten Hops* (under contract with University of Chicago Press).

Perry King is an author, freelance journalist, and strategic communications professional born and raised in the Greater Toronto Area. The son of immigrant parents, King has extensive reporting and storytelling experience, with a serious interest in sports, education, history, and urbanism. He has bylines with *Sportsnet*, *Spacing*, *Toronto Star*, *Globe and Mail*, and the BBC. A proud alumnus of the University of King's College, Halifax, he is the author of *Rebound: Sports, Community, and the Inclusive City* (Coach House Books, 2021).

Meegan Lim is an illustrator and arts facilitator, based in Brampton, Ontario, who strives to nurture community growth and healing through visual arts. She is known for her detailed illustrations focusing on food and cultural identity, and the vast stories within those intersections. She holds a Bachelor of Design in Illustration, specializing in Entrepreneurship and Social Innovation, from OCAD University.

Karon Liu has been a staff food reporter for the *Toronto Star* since 2015 and aims to link food with culture, history, identity, politics – anything you can imagine. He's also an avid home cook, and his favourite utensil is a pair of wooden chopsticks his grandma used to use

John Lorinc is a Toronto journalist and editor. He writes about urban affairs, climate, and business for a range of publications, including *Spacing*, the *Globe and Mail*, and the *Walrus*. He is the author of four books, including *Dream States* (Coach House Books, 2022) and has co-edited or project-managed five previous Coach House uTOpia anthologies.

Domenica Marchetti is the author of eight books on Italian home cooking. Her articles and recipes have been widely published in publications such as *Eating Well*, *Food & Wine*, *Washington Post*, and *La Cucina Italiana*. She teaches online cooking classes and leads occasional small-group tours and workshops in Italy. Visit her website at www.domenicacooks.com.

Angela Misri is an award-winning journalist, educator, and author of seven books, including *ValHamster, Pickles vs. the Zombies*, and the *Portia Adams Adventures*. Misri has worked as a digital journalist for twenty years at the CBC and the *Walrus* and is an assistant professor in the journalism department at Toronto Metropolitan University.

Miles Morrisseau (Métis Nation) graduated from the Program in Journalism for Native People at Western University in 1986. He was the National Native Affairs Broadcaster for CBC Radio and covered historic events, including the Oka Crisis and Elijah Harper's defeat of the Meech Lake Accord. He was editor in chief of *Indian Country Today*, the largest Native American newspaper in the U.S. He is currently special correspondent for ICTnews.

Matt Murtagh-Wu is and owns the Dumpling King, a local handmade frozen-dumpling company that sources its ingredients from Vancouver's Chinatown. Born of a father from Hong Kong and a mother from Victoria, BC, the Dumpling King hopes to express, both in his food and message, that celebrating heritage, identity, and ingredients on your own terms will always make something delicious. The Dumpling King can be found in the freezers of Vancouver's local cafés, lifestyle stores, and neighbourhood grocers.

Sylvia Putz is a huge fan of books, ideas, and culinary flavours of all sorts. She is a writer and communications specialist currently finishing a family memoir of her parents' experience growing up in wartime Germany. Sylvia lives in Toronto with her husband and two children. Each year she celebrates her birthday with a dim sum feast.

Amy Rosen is a James Beard–nominated, award-winning journalist and cookbook author whose work has appeared in *Bon Appétit, Food & Wine, enRoute,* and the *Globe and Mail.* She is the author of six cookbooks; her latest is *Canada's Best New Cookbook* (Spafax, 2022). She's also the owner of Rosen's Cinnamon Buns. (Did you see her on *Dragons' Den?*)

Bev Katz Rosenbaum is a Toronto-based freelance editor and a novelist for young people. Her most recent book is *I'm Good and Other Lies* (DCB, 2021), about a teen experiencing Toronto's first COVID-19-related lockdown. Bev has taught writing at Centennial College and worked as an editor for several book publishers and magazines. She lives for good meals with friends and family and is delighted to have had an opportunity to defend the humble krepele.

Michal Stein is a writer and podcast producer based in Toronto. Her work has appeared in the *Globe and Mail, Toronto Star,* FLARE, *Broadview,* and *McSweeney's Internet Tendency.* A vegetarian from age eleven to twenty-one, she first tried dim sum when she was twenty-two. She has never looked back.

Cheryl Thompson is an assistant professor in performance at the Creative School, Toronto Metropolitan University. She is the author of *Uncle: Race, Nostalgia, and the Politics of Loyalty* (Coach House Books, 2021) and *Beauty in a Box: Detangling the Roots of Canada's Black Beauty Culture* (Wilfrid Laurier University

Press, 2019). Cheryl is currently writing a book on the history of blackface in Canada.

Julie Van Rosendaal is an award-winning food journalist, writing primarily for the *Globe and Mail*. She's the author of twelve best-selling cookbooks (her latest is *Cookies I Have Loved*) and she talks about food weekly on the *Calgary Eyeopener* on CBC Radio.

Monika Warzecha is the digital editor at *The Walrus* and has contributed to the *Globe and Mail, Toronto Star,* TVO.org, and *Vice*. She is currently working on a collection of short stories about the Polish diaspora.

Typeset in Albertina, New Spirit, and Ganache.

Printed at the Coach House on bpNichol Lane in Toronto, Ontario, on Rolland paper. This book was printed with vegetable-based ink on a 1973 Heidelberg KORD offset litho press. Its pages were folded on a Baumfolder, gathered by hand, bound on a Sulby Auto-Minabinda, and trimmed on a Polar single-knife cutter.

Coach House is on the traditional territory of many nations including the Mississaugas of the Credit, the Anishnabeg, the Chippewa, the Haudenosaunee, and the Wendat peoples, and is now home to many diverse First Nations, Inuit, and Métis peoples. We acknowledge that Toronto is covered by Treaty 13 with the Mississaugas of the Credit. We are grateful to live and work on this land.

Edited for the press by John Lorinc
Cover design and interior illustrations by Meegan Lim
Interior design by Crystal Sikma

Coach House Books
80 bpNichol Lane
Toronto ON M5S 3J4
Canada

416 979 2217
800 367 6360

mail@chbooks.com
www.chbooks.com